SMOKE &FIRE

Recipes and Menus for Entertaining Outdoors

To Chloe, Jack, and Eliza—
I love and live to share every delicious
outdoor moment with you all.

The author's proceeds will be donated to Feeding America, serving over
46 million Americans in need with its nationwide network of member food banks.
www.feedingamerica.org

By HOLLY PETERSON

SMOKE & FIRE

Recipes and Menus for Entertaining Outdoors

Photographs by ROSS WHITAKER

ASSOULINE

CONTENTS

INTRODUCTION

Whether it's a full-blown lobster bake on the Atlantic shores, a surf-and-turf guys' night over a backyard open pit, or your kid's high school tailgate with a little hardware-store hibachi, fire-cooked food will make an occasion pop even louder than the embers before you.

Paleolithic cavemen must have figured this out around 300,000 years ago, when they first placed stones in a ring around a flame. A roast in the oven is lovely, but meat dripping from a spit, fish perfumed with smoke, and vegetables boasting those telltale grill marks are just fun-er to chomp. This book is a tool to create those moments, a lever, a springboard. A guide for the pit master, the hostess, and the outdoor entertainer, the recipes here are simple to prepare and geared toward several types of grills, outdoor ovens—and even your indoor kitchen. In *Smoke and Fire*, you'll learn how to add the aroma of wood chips to your tailgate pulled-chicken sliders; steam a lobster in the sand with coals, hot rocks, and salt water— and wine-soaked burlap; and bake the perfect triple berry cobbler right in the coals of your campfire—all delicious fare created with smoke and fire.

The word *focus* is derived from the Latin for *fireplace*, the focal point of any home for centuries. All elements of a fire plead to our senses: the hypnotizing rhythmic dancing of flames, the aromas wafting off as honey-covered ribs turn to candy, the butter bubbling on a row of grilled corn kernels, or the crisping of a chocolate chip cookie cooked in a cast-iron skillet over a moonlit flame.

The recipes in this book are curated from the accomplished professional chefs I'm lucky to consider friends and whose recipes are credited throughout: the South's truest gem, Julia Reed, and her friend Ryan Prewitt, exccutive chef—owner of Pêche Seafood Grill in New Orleans; Food Network's Katie Lee; the classically trained, can-do-all Tom Kukoly; big-sky Montana's Ben Jones; pizza expert Henry Margaritis; outdoor oven guru Warren Schierenbeck; and even my comedian friend Ali Wentworth, who shared her WASP crab dip. I love to cook, but these men and women are great artists who bring this book to the level you, the culinary enthusiast, deserve. They are masters of outdoor cooking and certainly great mentors of mine. Together we created these outdoor gatherings—events that pair sizzling food and conversation among family and friends. Please join us, and let me know how it goes.

Holly Peterson
Cooking@HollyPeterson.com

TIPS FOR COOKING WITH FIRE

Let the fire peak and the flames die down. You want a consistent, steady source of heat.

Cooking with fire is meant to be pure fun, so we've kept these recipes as simple, flavorful, and unfussy as they come. Use few ingredients and keep them fresh and local if possible. Most will work on your trusty Weber grill, but experiment with some of the outdoor cooking toys I've put together to add adventure to the experience. Last-minute weather patterns or kids' needs demand flexibility, so I've included information to make meals in your kitchen and indoor oven. And for the obsessive barbecuer—*you know who you are*—you'll find a wagon full of recipes, tips, and information to keep you reading up late at night.

Equipment, methods, tools, and cookware are all elements to consider when preparing food outdoors. When we cook with fire, we are not cooking over flames so much as cooking over heat. You need to allow time to let the fire peak and the flames die down, to create a consistent, steady source of heat for your food. In a charcoal chimney (Weber makes a good one), transforming lump charcoal (much better than briquettes) from black to ashen color takes about twenty-five minutes. Burning wood down to embers can take ninety minutes. The times for both can be looked at as "prep"—time you won't have to spend cleaning up a kitchen. Grab a colorful cocktail found in these pages and enjoy the sunset while your flames turn to embers.

In addition to the flame, there's the surface you are grilling on. It is most often a metal grate, but consider a slab of slate as they do in Andorra, on the southern border of France, endorsed by the greatest chef in New York, Eric Ripert. Cooking a steak *pierrade*, or "on stone," is an inexpensive and elegant idea.

Mexican Street Corn, page 122.

Food cooked in an outdoor oven, directly on coals, or on a woodpile must be placed in fireproof dishes and pans that won't crack or shatter. Cast-iron skillets work brilliantly on flames, in an outdoor oven, on top of hot box coals, and even on the grill. Terracotta and clay cookware also perform very well outdoors, and I've included my favorite brands on the following pages. You can even use disposable aluminum lasagna pans from the grocery store. They are supercheap and come in all shapes and sizes, and I use them in my outdoor pizza oven—where I'll cook a whole snapper stuffed with tomato, purple onion, basil, and olive oil. I use smaller aluminum pans right on my barbecue grill to keep food warm. For a perfect summer dessert, I even place peach halves in aluminum muffin tins until they char in spots, then add a dollop of ricotta and a drizzle of mint syrup.

ADDING FLAVOR WITH WOOD CHIPS

The flavor of your food will result partially from the heat source. So if you haven't considered your heat source as an ingredient, now's the time to start. Most of us use charcoal or gas for grill heat now, which can be enhanced with wood (chips, chunks, or even pellets) that adds aromas and flavors through smoke. Think of wood as a spice: It imparts flavors that range from subtle to smack-you-in-the-face. As with wine, you just have to try different varieties to figure out what you like.

Wood smoke can be almost any shade of gray, brown, black, yellow, or blue, depending on its particle size. Serious pit masters consider invisible smoke with a pale blue tint to be the pinnacle of perfection, but it's really only necessary for a low-and-slow barbecue, when meat is sitting on the grill for hours.

Common milder woods include apple, pear, cherry, or peach. They lend a light sweetness to delicate flesh such as fish. Apple can sweeten a nice ham and is subtle enough that it won't overpower poultry.

Moving up the spectrum of flavor intensity are oak, hickory, maple, and pecan. They all can handle beef, game, and larger cuts like pork shoulders and large briskets.

Mesquite is also very common, but it is by far the strongest wood. This is your ghost pepper of smoking woods. Do not overdo it. Don't throw mesquite on the grill if you're barbecuing ribs for hours until they fall off the bone, but do turn to it for a quick burst of flavor for meals that cook more quickly, like steaks. This acrid essence is not for everyone.

Want a little taste of tartness? You can soak wood chips in wine before putting them on the coals or in a smoker box. My friend John Markus, one of those hugely accomplished (and obsessive) grillers, advises soaking a handful of hay in bourbon and laying it right onto the coals to add a smoky, savory flavor to warmed oysters on the half shell.

OUTDOOR COOKING TOYS

Beyond the classic Weber Charcoal Kettle that took over America in the 1950s, its larger cousin, the Weber Ranch Kettle grill (great for larger cuts or multiple items), and dependable propane grills (convenient, but disdained by purists), there is a wide range of machines for outdoor cooking.

Hot Box

La Caja China, often referred to as a Caja (pronounced ka-ha) box, generates powerful radiant heat like an enclosed oven. Chinese migrants who came to Cuba as laborers in the mid-1800s constructed a similar box with a fire on top to roast their meat far more quickly than over an open flame. The coals lie on a grate on the top section (you can heat them in a charcoal chimney starter), heating the food placed underneath. The Caja box can hold a full clambake or a huge group of chickens and vegetables in a two-sided grate that locks on the edges for easy flipping. A sixty-pound hog will cook in less than four hours. The box comes with a metal rake to handle the hot coals and La Caja sells bear claws for turning whole chickens and large cuts of meat. Remember to place your Caja China box far away from your home, garage, shed, and other permanent structures to prevent fire accidents when the breeze blows.

Outdoor Pizza Oven

My own outdoor pizza oven has become the focal point of our home and all of the different kinds of entertaining we do on the back deck. A pizza oven sucks oxygen through the D-shaped opening in the front to feed the burning logs in the back, then releases it through the chimney. Both smaller, outdoor tabletop models and larger, professional-sized models are available. Don't forget to clean the chimney regularly.

We installed a version that is half-gas and half-wood, significantly reducing the heating time compared with an all wood–burning oven. I heat my Wood Stone model with gas flames that line the back for about a half hour and then throw three logs on to one side (they spontaneously combust with the roiling heat already present). Once the desired temperature is reached, we turn off the gas and just keep tending the wood, which makes us feel like authentic pilgrims, albeit in my case one in white jeans and a colored summer caftan.

Ceramic Cookers

A ceramic cooker is the most diverse cooker out there. You can slow-cook ribs on low heat in a ceramic cooker all night or fire it up to seven hundred degrees to sear steaks quickly. (At high heat you have to lift up the earthenware lid periodically to let the fire breathe.) You can also use them for many purposes besides grilling and smoking, such as making pizza and bread. The most famous is the Big Green Egg, with its iconic domed green lid. The Primo Ceramic Grill is also very good and made in America. The blinged-up version is the Kamado Cooker, with gorgeous tiles in every shade, from indigo to caramel to ivory.

Smokers

Anybody can grill a hot dog or a hamburger, but it takes a little more artistry to get a juicy brisket or ribs that are falling off the bone after hours cooked "low and slow." That may be why more Americans than ever are buying smokers. Models that burn wood logs are the most authentic and the most expensive.

Electric and affordable pellet smokers are popular for allowing you to "set it and forget it." You add wood chunks or chips to the charcoal smokers to achieve whatever tastes you want and can hang an entire turkey or a long rack of ribs vertically from hooks inside. Bradley smokers have a maximum temperature of 250 degrees and can be used as a slow cooker or a slow-roasting oven. They require very little attendance and give you control over how much smoke you want to use, how long you want to cook the food, and at what temperature.

Yoder smokers, which weigh more than twelve hundred pounds, are found at big competitions and are revered by the real masters. Those with money to spare go for models that look like trucks and trailers and fire-engine red race cars offered by Jambo Pits. Lang BBQ smokers are known for a reverse-flow design that has since been copied by competitors.

Meat Thermometer

Most grills and smokers include dial thermometers that can give wildly unpredictable reads that are off by as much as fifty or one hundred degrees. Instead, use a rapid-read food thermometer—such as Thermapen's Mk4, called the Lamborghini of instant-read thermometers—by sticking the probe in the side of the food an inch above the hot grate.

Maverick and iGrill make wireless and Bluetooth thermometers as well. Whether you are at your neighbor's house having a glass of wine and need to check on your Caja box chickens or starting a smoke at midnight and want to make sure all is going well at 3 a.m., it's a modern miracle to have the temperature on your phone.

Cookware

Be very careful when putting bakeware onto grills, glowing coals, a wood-fired flame, or in your outdoor oven. Dishes and pans can easily crack or explode if they're not made of the right material. Hard ceramics or enameled cast irons that work wonders inside have a five-hundred-degree limit—too low for a hot flame or the intense heat of a pizza oven—and Pyrex-type glass will shatter in extreme temperature changes and can't be placed on a direct flame. My favorite options are traditional cast iron from Lodge, terracotta from Forno Bravo, black clay cookware from La Chamba, and classic restaurant-style aluminum core (and even disposable aluminum baking dishes from the grocery store).

Scallions, for Herb-Roasted Salmon, page 19.

SUMMER SOLSTICE COCKTAIL PARTY

RECIPES
1. Crostini
   · Goat Cheese with Baby Carrots and Radishes
   · Roasted Broccolini and Ricotta
   · Crab and Corn
2. Fire-Roasted Chicken with Snow Peas and Gremolata
3. Herb-Roasted Salmon with Salsa Verde
4. Bacon-Wrapped Radicchio and Pear

DRINKS
5. Orange Iced Tea with Huckleberry Syrup
6. Pomegranate Tequila Punch
7. Mango Mimosas
8. Cucumber Martinis

Recipes by Warren Schierenbeck with pomegranate tequila punch by Tom Kukoly

Each drop of sweet peach juice or barbecue honey glaze reminds us that all of our senses are heightened in the heat of summer. This special season is heralded by the solstice on June 21, a term derived from the Latin *sol* (sun) and *sistere* (to stand still). It's no surprise we want those flavors to do just that: linger as long as possible.

The summer solstice is scientifically considered an instant in time, an infinitesimal tilt in the Earth's axis when we are most inclined toward the sun. Without the Earth spinning on that axis, we would have no seasons, no summer corn, and no frothy butter on bountiful grilled shellfish.

Cooking outside with the freshest local produce, fish, poultry, and meats is my way of making summer stand still and staving off the melancholy feeling that the season passes us by too quickly.

Mango Mimosas, page 25.

Crostini

Serves 36

| 12 loaves artisanal bread | Salt and freshly ground | *Crostini toppings |
| Olive oil | black pepper | |

- Preheat your indoor or outdoor oven to 350°F.
- Slice bread and arrange on a baking sheet. Drizzle with olive oil and sprinkle with salt and pepper.
- Toast in oven, turning once, until each side is golden brown, about 6 minutes.
- Top as desired.

  TIP: Bread for crostini can also be toasted directly on the grill.

* Crostini Toppings

Goat Cheese with Baby Carrots and Radishes

| 1 bunch assorted baby carrots | 2 cups soft goat cheese, | Salt |
| 2 bunches assorted radishes | such as chèvre | Extra-virgin olive oil |

- Slice baby carrots and radishes and soak in ice water to clean. Drain and pat dry.
- Smear toasted crostini with goat cheese, and pile a small amount of mixed carrots and radishes on top. Finish with salt and olive oil.

Roasted Broccolini and Ricotta

| 2 bunches broccolini | Salt and freshly ground | 2 cups whole-milk ricotta cheese |
| Olive oil | black pepper | 2 lemons, cut in half |

- Preheat oven or grill to 350°F. Spread broccolini on a rimmed baking sheet and drizzle with olive oil. Bake or grill until charred and wilted, about 10 minutes.
- Transfer to a bowl and cover to steam. When it reaches room temperature, roughly chop the broccolini and season with salt and pepper.
- Smear ricotta on crostini. Place a small pile of chopped broccolini on top, then give each a squeeze of fresh lemon and a drizzle of olive oil.

Crab and Corn

2 ears corn	1 tsp Old Bay seasoning	1 Tbsp chopped cilantro
8 oz lump crabmeat, picked	2 Tbsp mayonnaise	2 limes, cut in half
clean of shells		

- Preheat grill or oven to 350°F. Grill or roast corn in husks until the husks turn black.
- Let corn steam in husks. Peel when they reach room temperature and slice the kernels off cobs.
- Combine corn, crab, Old Bay, mayonnaise, and cilantro. Fold gently, and squeeze limes over salad.
- Pile salad on crostini.

Fire-Roasted Chicken with Snow Peas and Gremolata

Serves 8 to 10

2 whole chickens, cut into 10 pieces (have your butcher do this)
1 cup chopped Italian flat-leaf parsley

Grated zest of 2 lemons
Olive oil
Salt and freshly ground black pepper
2 cups snow peas

1 cup breadcrumbs (pulse leftover crostini in a food processor)
1 cup basil leaves

- Preheat outdoor oven to medium or indoor oven to 450°F. Spread chicken pieces on a rimmed baking sheet and season liberally with parsley, lemon zest, olive oil, salt, and pepper.
- Place in outdoor oven for 20 minutes or indoor oven for 35 minutes, or until chicken is mahogany brown.
- Scatter snow peas, breadcrumbs, and basil over chicken and bake for 10 more minutes.
- Arrange on a platter and pour all the delicious juices over the chicken to serve.

Herb-Roasted Salmon with Salsa Verde

Serves 12

*Salsa Verde

1 cup chopped parsley
1 cup chopped cilantro
1/2 cup chopped mint

1/4 cup capers, minced
4 anchovies, chopped
2 cloves garlic, minced

3 cups extra-virgin olive oil
Salt and freshly ground black pepper

*Salmon

12 (5-oz) salmon filets, skinned and boned
6 lemons, cut in half

1 bunch spring onions or scallions, roots removed
1 cup extra-virgin olive oil

Salt and freshly ground black pepper

- Make the salsa verde: Mince herbs, capers, anchovies, and garlic together until it forms a fine paste. Mix in olive oil to reach about the consistency of pesto and season with salt and pepper. I prefer to cut everything by hand; it adds that rustic, handmade feel and marries the flavors that much better.
- Prepare the salmon: Preheat outdoor oven to medium or indoor oven to 450°F.
- Rub half of the salsa verde on the salmon filets and place them on a rimmed baking sheet or terracotta dish. Scatter lemon halves and spring onions around the fish. Drizzle with olive oil and season with salt and pepper.
- Bake outdoors for 9 minutes or indoors for 12 minutes, or until salmon is flaky and still pink in the middle.
- Serve with the remaining salsa verde.

Bacon-Wrapped Radicchio and Pear

Serves 16

4 heads radicchio
2 ripe Bosc pears
1 lb bacon

¼ cup sugar
Salt and freshly ground
  black pepper

Olive oil
½ cup honey
½ cup balsamic vinegar

- Preheat grill or outdoor oven to medium, or indoor oven to 450°F.
- Cut each radicchio into 4 wedges, keeping the stems intact. Slice pears into wedges and remove seeds.
- Place one wedge of pear on top of each wedge of radicchio and wrap together with bacon; place in a cast-iron pan (no bacon on the grill!).
- Sprinkle with sugar, salt, pepper, and olive oil.
- Grill or bake until bacon is crispy and radicchio is charred.
- Remove and drizzle with honey and balsamic vinegar to serve.

DRINKS

Orange Iced Tea with Huckleberry Syrup

Serves 5

1 pint overripe huckleberries
  or blackberries
1 cup sugar
2 Tbsp freshly squeezed
  lemon juice

Orange pekoe tea, or your
  favorite variety
1 orange, sliced

- Make the huckleberry syrup: Bring berries, sugar, lemon juice, and 1 cup water to a boil in saucepot. Set aside to steep and cool.
- Make the tea: Brew your favorite tea according to your preference. Let it cool.
- To serve, pour the tea into a large pitcher or glasses; add ice, orange slices, and ¼ cup huckleberry syrup to the pitcher or 1 tablespoon to each glass.

TIP: Refrigerate the huckleberry syrup in an airtight glass jar, and it should last for two to three weeks of great drinks! It's also a great addition to pancakes.

Set up the bar early. People like to serve themselves and make drinks the way they like. The host sets the tone, so relax and let your guests do the same.

As a cardinal rule, I bring food out early, about thirty minutes after the party begins. I'd love to start a movement suggesting every host do the same. No one wants to stand for an hour hungry and a little too tipsy. If you bring out the food, your guests feel in control of the night. With a full plate, people are satiated, happy, and staying because they want to, not because they are waiting for food. Try it. I promise it makes for a buzzier, cheerier party.

Pomegranate Tequila Punch

Serves 12 to 15

1 bottle blanco tequila
1 bottle chilled Champagne or
    sparkling wine
4 cups cranberry juice

2 ½ cups grapefruit juice
1 cup honey
1 cup pomegranate seeds

4 limes, sliced
1 ruby red grapefruit or
    2 oranges, sliced

- Mix all ingredients and serve super chilled with lots of ice.

Mango Mimosas

Serves 5

1 cup mango purée
½ cup freshly squeezed
    orange juice

2 Tbsp freshly squeezed
    lime juice

1 bottle Champagne or
    sparkling wine, chilled
1 lime, sliced, for garnish

- Combine mango purée, orange juice, and lime juice in small pitcher.
- Fill glasses two-thirds full of very cold sparkling wine and top with juice mixture.
- Garnish with lime slices and enjoy!

Cucumber Martinis

Serves 5

16 oz vodka
¾ cup freshly squeezed
    lime juice

½ cup simple syrup
8 mint leaves
15 cucumber slices, for garnish

To make simple syrup, place equal amounts sugar and water in a pot; bring to a boil, then set aside to cool.

- Combine vodka, lime juice, simple syrup, and mint leaves in a cocktail shaker.
- Add ice and shake until cold.
- Strain into chilled martini glasses and garnish with cucumber.

EAST END LOBSTER BAKE

When it comes to outdoor cooking, I like to go big on the beach. Since I surf with family and friends alike, perhaps my extra zeal for shoreline entertaining is an homage to the ocean that provides us all so much joy.

For this lobster bake, we wanted to eat before sunset, so we raced to the beach at about 3 p.m. to start digging the fire pit. Once the stones and wood were hot, we placed lobsters, clams, mussels, and corn on top in stages and covered the prize with burlap soaked in the sea. With the tables set, I had some time alone to sit on the Atlantic shoreline and sip the perfect white sangria (page 34).

The guests arrived on the beach in very game family groupings saddled with blanket- and windbreaker-filled tote bags. It isn't simple for anyone to crack open hard lobster claws, dig out the meat, and dunk it in butter that's still hot while the sun is setting and the wind is beginning to cool the air. That's why I make lists and prepare extra carefully for any event in the sand.

A beach lobster bake takes time and effort to prepare, but the effects linger. From the smoky smell on your sweatshirt to the stubborn gooey marshmallow on your jeans, through October or even years later, when you remember this particular summer, it'll be one of the first visions that pop into your mind.

When European settlers first reached North America, lobsters stacked two feet high on the shores greeted them. Seen back then as the "cockroaches of the sea," they were relegated to prison gruel or fertilizer. As time went by, lobster was tinned as a cheap source of protein. By the mid-1800s, non–New Englanders had grown to like the hearty lobster meat they tasted in tin cans, and soon it became the delicacy that stands today as a centerpiece of an outdoor event.

RECIPES
1. Lobster Bake with Littleneck Clams and Mussels
2. Strip Steaks Grilled Beachside with Chimichurri
3. Long Island Asparagus with Shaved Manchego and Peaches
4. Grilled Potato Skins with Sour Cream, Bacon, and Jalapeño

DRINK
5. White Sangria

DESSERT
6. Strawberry Griddle Cakes with Honey

Recipes by Tom Kukoly

Pour a bottle of beer or a glass or two of white wine directly on the burlap bake and let the steam flavor the food.

Lobster Bake with Littleneck Clams and Mussels

Serves 8 to 10

✳Lobster Bake Setup

10–15 medium-size river rocks
20 lbs firewood
20 lbs rockweed (seaweed)

Burlap
Painter's canvas (from hardware or art store)

✳Ingredients

8 (1½-lb) lobsters
1 bushel (10 lbs) littleneck clams
1 bushel (10 lbs) mussels

10 ears corn (in husk)
1 lb (4 sticks) unsalted butter, melted

- Dig a hole in the sand 2 feet deep, 3 feet wide, and 4 feet long.
- Line hole with rocks, and build a wood fire on top. Let it burn for about 3 hours, until coals are hot with no flames.
- Cover the rocks and coals with half of the seaweed. Add a layer of wet burlap, preferably moistened in the sea.
- Place lobsters, clams, mussels, and corn on top of the burlap.
- Cover with another layer of wet burlap, the remaining seaweed, and a wet painter's canvas.
- Leave for 1 hour, drink a few beers, and your lobster bake is ready! Serve with melted butter.

①Strip Steaks Grilled Beachside with Chimichurri

Serves 8 to 10

½ cup olive oil
1 cup cilantro leaves
8 cloves garlic
1 tsp crushed red pepper flakes

¼ cup white vinegar
Freshly squeezed juice of 1 orange
Freshly squeezed juice of 1 lime

Salt and freshly ground black pepper
6 (12-oz) strip steaks

- Make the chimichurri sauce: Combine all the ingredients except the steaks, and let rest for 1 hour.
- Grill the steaks to your liking.
- Let rest for 10 minutes, then slice in strips and serve with chimichurri.

② Long Island Asparagus with Shaved Manchego and Peaches

Serves 8 to 10

3 bunches asparagus

6 ripe peaches, pitted and sliced thin

2 Tbsp olive oil
8 oz Manchego cheese, shaved

- Prepare a grill. Brush asparagus and peaches with olive oil. Grill for about 3 to 5 minutes.
- Serve on platter with shaved Manchego cheese.

①

②

③

③ Grilled Potato Skins with Sour Cream, Bacon, and Jalapeño

Serves 8 to 10

10 small Yukon Gold potatoes
5 jalapeño peppers, halved lengthwise and seeded

16 oz bacon
2 Tbsp olive oil
1 cup sour cream

Chopped cilantro
Salt and freshly ground black pepper

- Prepare a bed of hot coals in a grill or campfire. Wrap potatoes individually in aluminum foil, and place on coals. Cook for 45 minutes, turning frequently, until cooked but still firm.
- Meanwhile, cook jalapeños and bacon in a cast-iron skillet on the grill. Chop them roughly.
- Slice potatoes in half and brush with olive oil. Cook on the grill grate until golden brown.
- Arrange on a platter and top with sour cream.
  Sprinkle with bacon and jalapeños, cilantro, and salt and pepper to taste.

A beach lobster bake takes time and effort to prepare, but the effects linger. Years later, when you remember this particular summer, it'll be one of the first visions that pop in your mind.

I prefer potatoes grilled and crunchy over boiled. Keep them out of the burlap bake.

LOBSTER BEACH LIST

Stick Lighter
Flashlights (15?)
Extra Long BBQ tools
Oven Mitts
Small Pan to Melt Butter
Dipping Containers for Butter
Small food testing table
Cutting Board
Big Knives to split Lobsters
Hammer
Real forks and knives
Glasses
Laterns / Oil Filled?
Tiki torches
Fire starters + wood
WEBER + Coal + starter
Wipes for Hands + Towels
Beach Chairs for Bonfire

WINE OPENER !!

LOBSTER BEACH LIST:

Stick Lighter
Flashlights . (x5)
Extra Long BBQ tools
Oven Mitts
Small Pan to Melt Butter
Dipping Containers for Butter
Small food testing table
Cutting Board
Big Knives to split Lobsters
Hammer
Real forks and knives
Glasses
Laterns / OIL filled!
Tiki torches
Fire starters + wood
WEBER + Coal + Starter
Wipes for Hands / Howels.
Beach Chairs for Bonfire

WINE OPENER !!

OTHER ITEMS TO REMEMBER FOR THE BEACH

- S'mores sticks
- Bucket to douse burning embers in salt water
- Don't forget to check each beach location's rules about fires and putting them out.

White Sangria

Serves 8 to 10

½ cup sugar
A few capfuls of vanilla extract, or scrapings from a split pod
4 ½ oz Grand Marnier
3 ripe peaches, pitted and sliced

2 pears or green apples, sliced
1 pint raspberries
½ cup sliced strawberries
½ cup pomegranate seeds
1 lemon, sliced

1 lime, sliced
1 bottle very cold dry white wine
1 bottle very cold Champagne or sparkling wine
1 cup club soda

- In a large pitcher, combine sugar, vanilla, and Grand Marnier, and stir until sugar dissolves.
- Add fruit, followed by white wine; chill for at least 30 minutes.
- Add sparkling wine and club soda before serving.

TIP: When making sangria, do not add ice, it will dilute the finished product too much. The key is to use lots of fruits, stir, and enjoy!

DESSERT

Strawberry Griddle Cakes with Honey

Serves 8 to 10

1 cup (2 sticks) unsalted butter, at room temperature, plus 4 tablespoons for the pan
1 cup plus 1 tablespoon sugar
4 eggs

1 cup sour cream
1 tsp vanilla extract
3 ¾ cups cake flour
1 ½ Tbsp baking powder

1 tsp salt
2 lbs strawberries, sliced
Honey (optional)
Vanilla ice cream (optional)

- Cream 1 cup butter and the sugar together with an electric mixer. Blend in eggs one at a time, then add sour cream and vanilla; beat 3 minutes. Slowly add flour, baking powder, and salt.
- Melt 4 tablespoons butter in a 10-inch cast-iron skillet. Put sliced strawberries in the skillet and pour batter over berries until pan is about half filled.
- Place skillet in oven at 375°F for about 45 minutes.
- At the beach, reheat on the grill.
- Serve from skillet drizzled with honey or topped with ice cream kept chilled in a cooler.

TIP: Start this recipe at home, as it's too messy for the beach.

JULIA REED'S LOUISIANA SHRIMP BOIL

Julia Reed earned her first paycheck taking coats at her parents' massive parties in the Mississippi Delta, where restaurants were few, cooking was of paramount importance, and giving a party was as natural as breathing. Early on, the revered, adored author and cook eavesdropped from behind bushes at her mother's birthday, graduation, wedding, and book parties that unfolded—often last minute and for huge crowds—inside and outside the family's home. These triumphs inspired Julia's famous recipes, which adhere to her mama's voice in her head: "Why don't you give them something that just tastes really good." Amen.

The Delta's rural and spread-out area injected family parties with spontaneity—people would constantly show up with a guitar or start mixing their favorite drink. "My firm belief," Julia says, "is that every really sexy party should have some danger, the possibility of a love affair, or sparks flying—in the figurative sense, not only the literal sense of this book—which is why cooking with fire is my kind of shindig."

Julia says one of the best things about her current hometown, New Orleans, is the "ridiculous abundance" of shellfish, like the gorgeous Gulf shrimp and oysters featured in her recipes here.

Julia's Louisiana Shrimp Boil is the easiest way to entertain outdoors for two people or one hundred, served over newspapers on a sandbar in the middle of the Mississippi River with coolers full of cold beer, or, as on this glorious summer day, in a courtyard off Religion Street with my favorite ice-cold Red Stripe beer.

Fried Oysters

Serves 14 to 16

1 pint fresh-shucked oysters
1 ¹/₂ cups white cornmeal or
    unseasoned Zatarain's Fish Fri
1 tsp salt, plus more to season

4 cups peanut oil
Freshly ground black pepper
Toast, for serving
✱ Tartar Sauce

- Drain the oysters. Add the teaspoon of salt to the cornmeal or Fish Fri and spread the mixture on a cookie sheet. Dredge the oysters in the cornmeal, one at a time, and place in a colander, shaking off any excess.

- Heat the peanut oil in a deep skillet over medium heat until it reaches 350°F. (You can check by sprinkling some of the cornmeal in the oil. If it spins and dances, the oil should be ready.) Gently drop an oyster into the hot oil. If it does not rise to the top, wait a minute or two and try again. If it does, add 3 to 4 more oysters, being careful not to crowd the pan. Cook the oysters, turning frequently. When the oysters are a light brown, remove them with a slotted spoon to paper towels to drain, and sprinkle with salt and pepper to taste.

- As soon as all the oysters are done, place on toasts spread with tartar sauce. Serve immediately.

✱ Tartar Sauce

2 large egg yolks
2 Tbsp freshly squeezed
    lemon juice
2 tsp Dijon mustard
¹/₂ tsp salt
1 ¹/₂ cups safflower or
    vegetable oil

2 Tbsp finely chopped parsley
2 Tbsp finely chopped chives
1 Tbsp finely chopped tarragon
    (optional)
2 Tbsp capers, roughly chopped
2 Tbsp finely chopped gherkin
    pickles or cornichons

6 scallions, with some of the
    tender green stalks included,
    finely chopped
Generous pinch of cayenne
    pepper

- Start by making a mayonnaise: In a large mixing bowl, hand-whisk together the egg yolks, lemon juice, Dijon, and salt, until smooth. Still whisking, slowly drizzle in the oil until the mayonnaise gets thick and the oil is easily incorporated. At this point, add the rest of the oil in a thin stream. If it gets too thick, add a teaspoon or so of warm water.

- Combine the mayonnaise with the herbs, capers, pickles, scallions, and cayenne.

✎ *TIP:* If you're too rushed to make homemade mayonnaise, you can always grab some from the store. Use about 1 ²/₃ cups, and stir in the remaining ingredients.

Louisiana Shrimp Boil

Serves 14 to 16

6 yellow onions, halved
12 cloves garlic
4 stalks celery, cut in
    2-inch pieces
4 lemons, halved

4 bags Zatarain's Crab Boil
1 Tbsp salt
1 tsp cayenne pepper
6 bay leaves
3 lbs red new potatoes

8 ears fresh corn, cut in half
2 lbs andouille sausage, sliced
    $1/2$-inch slices
4 lbs large shrimp, unpeeled
Hot sauce, for serving

- Fill a large pot with 8 quarts of water and bring to a boil on a propane burner. Add the onions, garlic, celery, lemons, Zatarain's Crab Boil, salt, cayenne, and bay leaves.

- Add the potatoes and cook for 10 minutes, until almost tender. Add the corn and sausage and cook 8 minutes more.

- Add the shrimp and turn off heat. Let mixture sit for about 10 minutes so that the shrimp can absorb the flavors; then drain or remove potatoes, corn, sausage, and shrimp with a slotted spoon.

- Serve your shrimp boil Southern style, on newspaper-covered picnic tables. Use your hands and dig in.

TIP: If you can't find andouille, you can substitute another flavorful sausage, like kielbasa.

Ryan Prewitt's
Smoked Tuna Dip

Makes about 5 cups

1 lb tuna
2 Tbsp Creole seasoning,
    such as Zatarain's
2 tsp salt, for rub
$1/2$ large onion, finely diced
1 stalk celery, minced
2 large scallions, thinly sliced

1 jalapeño pepper, stemmed,
    seeded, and diced
$1/2$ cup mayonnaise
$1/2$ cup sour cream
2 Tbsp Creole mustard
1 Tbsp prepared horseradish
1 Tbsp hot sauce, such as Tabasco

$1/2$ tsp Worcestershire sauce
1 tsp kosher salt
$1/2$ tsp freshly ground black pepper
$1/2$ tsp paprika
Zest and juice of 1 lemon
Crackers, for serving

- Season the tuna with Creole seasoning and 2 teaspoons salt. Marinate overnight, uncovered, in the refrigerator.

- Heat charcoal grill to 275°F. Throw a handful of wood chips on the coals, and place the tuna on the cooler side of the cooker. Smoke until the tuna is well done and breaks apart easily, about 25 minutes.

- Break the fish into small pieces. Combine all the remaining ingredients in a mixing bowl; taste and adjust seasonings, adding more lemon, hot sauce, or salt and pepper as desired. Allow to sit for a few hours or overnight to allow the flavors to come together.

- Serve with crackers.

❝ *I grew up in the Mississippi Delta, which is rural and spread out. Every party had elements of spontaneity—you never knew who would come with a guitar or start mixing up some of their favorite drinks. My firm belief is that every really sexy party should have an element of danger, which is why cooking with fire is my kind of shindig.* **❞**

JULIA REED

43

Satsuma Orange Old Fashioned

Serves 1

1 sugar cube (preferably
   Perruche)
3–4 dashes Peyshaud's bitters
   or Fee Brothers Old Fashion
   Aromatic Bitters

2 dashes Fee Brothers
   Orange Bitters
2 slices satsuma orange
3 oz bourbon
1 Luxardo maraschino cherry,
   for garnish

- Put the sugar cube, both bitters, and 1 ounce cold water in the bottom of the highball glass. Using a muddler or small wooden spoon, muddle the ingredients. Add one of the citrus slices and continue to muddle for a bit longer.

- Fill glass with ice. Add bourbon, stir well, and garnish with the remaining satsuma slice and Luxardo cherry.

Satsuma Orange-Gin Coolers with Rosemary Syrup

Serves 6

1 cup simple syrup (page 25)
1 bunch rosemary, plus
   branches for garnish
6 oz gin, chilled

6 oz freshly squeezed satsuma
   orange juice, strained and chilled
Freshly grated lime zest

You can use clementines, tangerines, or whatever orange is in season instead of satsumas.

- Heat the simple syrup to boiling; remove from heat. Add a handful of rosemary branches (reserving some for garnish) to the syrup and let steep for 30 minutes to an hour. Remove branches and strain syrup; this will keep, refrigerated, for a month.

- Put the gin in glasses and add orange juice. Stir in 1 to 2 teaspoons rosemary simple syrup, or to taste. Grate lime zest over the top and garnish with rosemary sprigs and ice.

Bananas Foster

Serves 4

4 Tbsp (½ stick) unsalted
    butter, at room temperature
1 cup packed brown sugar

½ tsp cinnamon
¼ cup banana liqueur
4 bananas, halved lengthwise

4 scoops vanilla ice cream
¼ cup white rum

- Stir together the butter, brown sugar, and cinnamon. Pour into a medium skillet over low heat. Cook, stirring constantly until sugar is dissolved. Stir in liqueur, add the banana pieces, and cook until lightly browned.

- Meanwhile, place a scoop of ice cream in each of four serving dishes. Pour the rum into a heated ladle and ignite it very carefully. When the flames die down, pour the rum into the skillet and stir.

- Place banana pieces over the ice cream, top with the warm rum sauce, and serve immediately.

TIP: If you want to double the recipe to serve eight, you'll need two skillets to keep it all warm at once.

66 *This recipe is adapted from Brennan's restaurant in New Orleans, where Bananas Foster was invented. I am sure I've never ignited the rum in the ladle—that's a waiter's trick to add drama tableside. I usually just light the whole damn skillet up. Up to you! Either way, it's easy and delicious.* 99

JULIA REED

CUBAN NIGHT IN A VINEYARD

Chefs Henry Margaritis and Tom Kukoly.

RECIPES
1. La Caja Box-Roasted Chicken with Sour Orange-Garlic Sauce
2. Coal-Roasted Atlantic Grouper Wrapped in Banana Leaves with Salsa Roja
3. Yellow Rice with Black Beans and Sweet Plantains
4. Avocado-Mango Salad with Bacon and Toasted Pumpkin Seeds
5. Grilled Zucchini with Pickled Red Onions, Peas, and Feta Cheese

DRINK
6. Blackberry-Lime Mojitos

DESSERT
7. Summer Berry Pecan Crumble

Recipes by Tom Kukoly

Last summer, I discovered a surefire way to enjoy my friends without having to spend too much time tending flames and food. To relish the waning summer sunset and to savor the blackberry mojito in your hand—all while cooking your food outdoors—consider buying a La Caja China box (page 11).

As Labor Day approached, my friend Tom Kukoly and I planned a Cuban sunset evening at Duck Walk Vineyards on Long Island. Tom is a fabulous chef from Georgia, classically trained in Europe but specializing in flexibility and outdoor whimsy. While we tasted delicious local wine varieties, the owners allowed us to place the Caja box on the safe cement back area and let our sour orange and garlic–infused chickens roast away until the color matched the glowing warm August sky.

La Caja Box-Roasted
Chicken with
Sour Orange-Garlic Sauce

Serves 8 to 10

4 farm-raised chickens
Salt and freshly ground
   black pepper
$\frac{1}{2}$ cup finely chopped cilantro

6 cloves garlic, crushed to a paste
   or minced
1 serrano pepper, finely chopped
1 cup freshly squeezed
   orange juice

Juice of 1 lemon
1 cup extra-virgin olive oil
2 oz Grand Marnier

- Split the chickens down the backbone and season with salt and pepper.
- Place chickens in a La Caja box and roast according to La Caja instructions. Alternatively, roast in a roasting pan in a preheated oven at 400°F, 45 minutes to 1 hour.
- Place cilantro, garlic, and serrano pepper in a bowl and whisk in orange juice, lemon juice, olive oil, and Grand Marnier. Season with salt to taste. Place chicken on serving platter, and spoon on the sauce.

TIP: When cooking with the La Caja box, let it do double-duty: You can reheat or cook in cast-iron skillets directly on the coals on top of the box.

OUTDOOR WINES

There actually is such a thing as outdoor wine. When dining alfresco, don't pop your best bottles or serve older or more delicate wines, because the nose, the sensual essence of the wine, gets diminished in the wind. David Sokolin, president of Sokolin Fine Wine Merchants, recommends hearty red wines like Brunello, young Bordeaux, and Châteauneuf du Pape or other grenache. For something lighter, try a pinot noir. For whites, consider a chardonnay or a sauvignon blanc, such as Sancerre or Pouilly Fumé. Then there's always rosé, perfect for long, lazy lunches when you want to pretend you're lounging in the Provençal sunshine.

Coal-Roasted Atlantic Grouper Wrapped in Banana Leaves with Salsa Roja

Serves 8

✳ Salsa Roja

4 Roma tomatoes, halved
   and seeded
2 serrano peppers, halved
   and seeded

1 white onion, cut into
   2-inch dice
3 cloves garlic

1 cup chopped cilantro
2 tsp salt
$\frac{1}{2}$ cup extra-virgin olive oil

✳ Grouper

8 (6-oz) grouper filets
Salt and freshly ground
   black pepper

8 banana leaves, cut into
   6-by-6-inch squares

- Make the salsa: Before leaving home, place the tomatoes, peppers, onion, and whole garlic cloves on a rimmed baking sheet, and roast in the oven at 400°F for 20 minutes; let cool.

- Put the cilantro, salt, and olive oil in a food processor. Add vegetables and pulse to blend. Pack in a tightly sealed container.

- Prepare the fish: If cooking indoors, preheat oven to 400°F. If cooking outdoors, prepare a bed of coals in a grill or campfire.

- Season filets with salt and pepper. Place 1 tablespoon salsa roja on each banana leaf, then place 1 grouper filet on top. Fold corners of the banana leaf to the center so they overlap, enclosing the filet in a tightly sealed package. Flip over so banana leaf corners are facing down.

- Place in a cast-iron skillet over coals and cook for 10 minutes.

- Serve with the remaining salsa roja.

✎ *TIP:* Make the salsa roja at home in a food processor.

> " *This traditional cooking method ensures the natural juices of the meal are locked inside the banana leaf. Here, you're cooking the fish in its own package which keeps it tight and steaming in delicious sauce.* "

TOMKUKOLY

Yellow Rice with Black Beans and Sweet Plantains

Serves 8 to 10

✳Black Beans

1 cup dried black beans	2 Tbsp sugar	Salt and freshly ground
1 onion, chopped	1 tsp ground cumin	black pepper
3 cloves garlic, chopped	1 bay leaf	

- Place beans in a pot and cover with 2 cups water. Bring to a boil.
  Remove from heat and set pot aside, covered, for 3 hours. Drain beans.
- In a separate pot, place onions, garlic, sugar, cumin, and bay leaf, and cook lightly.
  Add beans and 3 cups water. Bring to a simmer. Cook for about 1 hour, until beans are tender.
- Drain beans, then season to taste with salt and pepper.

✳Yellow Rice

2 Tbsp olive oil	2 cups long-grain white rice	Salt and freshly ground
1/2 cup chopped onion	2 tsp ground turmeric	black pepper
2 cloves garlic, chopped		

- Place olive oil, onion, garlic, and rice in a large stockpot. Sauté lightly until rice is translucent,
  then add turmeric. Add water to 1 inch above the rice. Simmer for about 20 minutes.
  Season with salt and pepper to taste.
- Mix beans and rice together and set aside. Rice and beans can be reheated before serving.

✳Sweet Plantains

2 Tbsp unsalted butter	1 Tbsp packed brown sugar	4 ripe sweet plantains, peeled,
2 Tbsp olive oil		left whole

- Place butter, olive oil, brown sugar, and plantains in a frying pan.
  Cook until plantains are golden brown.
- Slice into 2-inch pieces and serve with rice and beans.

I vote bright hues and tones everywhere when entertaining outdoors. Color is festive and makes everyone happier from the moment they walk up and grab that first blackberry mojito.

Avocado-Mango Salad with Bacon and Toasted Pumpkin Seeds

Serves 8 to 10

8 oz bacon

¼ cup lime juice

¼ cup olive oil

1 Tbsp honey

1 Tbsp Dijon mustard

1 Tbsp white sugar

Salt and freshly ground
black pepper

1 cup pumpkin seeds

6 avocados

2 large mangoes

4 cups arugula

- Cook bacon until crispy, then crumble.
- Whisk lime juice, olive oil, honey, mustard, sugar, salt, and pepper in a small bowl.
- Toast pumpkin seeds in a dry medium-hot pan for about 90 seconds, browning them slightly.
- Slice avocados and mangoes into 1-inch pieces. Toss in a large bowl, and mix in arugula and dressing. Add crispy bacon and toasted pumpkin seeds to serve.

Grilled Zucchini with Pickled Red Onions, Peas, and Feta Cheese

Serves 8 to 10

½ cup white wine vinegar

1 tsp sugar

1 red onion, thinly sliced into rings

6 zucchini

1 lb fresh peas

Salt

1 ½ cups crumbled feta cheese

- Whisk vinegar and sugar in a small bowl, and add the onions. Let marinate for 30 minutes, then drain.
- Meanwhile, split the zucchini lengthwise, brush with olive oil, and grill over high heat until cooked. Let cool, then slice into 2-inch pieces.
- Cook the peas in salted boiling water for 2 minutes.
- In a bowl, toss zucchini, peas, and feta together.
- Place on a platter and top with onions to serve.

Blackberry-Lime Mojitos

Serves 8 to 10

1 cup freshly squeezed lime juice

1 cup simple syrup (page 25)

2 cups white rum

16 oz fresh blackberries

1 full handful fresh mint

12 oz club soda

1 lime, thinly sliced, for garnish

- Combine lime juice, simple syrup, and rum in a large pitcher.
- Coarsely chop half the blackberries and mint. Place the mixture inside pitcher and stir.
- Serve over ice and top off with a shot of club soda.
- Garnish with the remaining blackberries and mint, plus the sliced lime.

For a late summer outdoor event, it's always refreshing to serve bright, chilled cocktails jammed with fruit and fresh herbs.

DESSERT

Summer Berry Pecan Crumble

Serves 8 to 10

✳ Crumble Topping

1 cup (2 sticks) unsalted butter, at room temperature

2 cups granulated sugar

1 cup chopped pecans

1 cup all-purpose flour

✳ Berry Filling

1 cup whole blackberries

1 cup whole raspberries

1 cup whole blueberries

1 cup whole strawberries

1 1/2 cups confectioners' sugar

1/4 cup cornstarch

1/2 cup (1 stick) unsalted butter

- Make the topping: Preheat oven to 350°F. Combine butter with the sugar, pecans, and flour, and mix until it has a sandy consistency.
- Spread evenly on a baking dish, and bake for 15 minutes, or until golden brown. Set aside to cool. Crumble into a container.
- Make the filling: Combine the berries with the confectioners' sugar, cornstarch, and butter in a pot. Bring to boil, stirring consistently until mixture thickens. Turn heat down to low and simmer for 1 hour. Reheat on coals in a cast-iron skillet. Top with pecan crumble.

PIZZA PARTY WITH CHEF HENRI

It all started with one simple quest: my desire to create the best wood-fired Neapolitan pizza in my home. As my kids have grown older, and just as they are trying to run out the back door, I've had to find clever ways to lure them back—like bugs to a porch light. My answer: a big outdoor pizza oven in my backyard.

My friend Henry Margaritis (nicknamed with French flair Henri) has had the same drive to perfect those pizzas we taste only in Italy. The chef and his father, Albert, helped discover and install the perfect combination wood-and-gas outdoor oven on my deck. The three of us even enrolled in the three-day Neapolitan Pizza School in California, run by the American Delegation of the Associazione Vera Pizza Napoletana, which gives special designation to pizzerias that meet strict requirements respecting the art of Neapolitan pizza making.

Henry and I have tried and tested various pizza doughs with different flours and yeasts to find quick and easy recipes using your outdoor pizza oven or a stone on your indoor oven rack. Henry, the patient professional, made pies for a kids' pizza party, and he shares our tried and true lessons here.

The kids always prepare better pizzas than the grown-ups—they have an innate understanding of simplicity.

RECIPES
1. Pizza Dough
2. Tomato Sauce
  ✳ Pizza Five Ways
3. Margherita
4. Mixed Mushroom, Caramelized Onion, and Fontina
5. Farm Stand Vegetable
6. Prosciutto and Arugula
7. White Zucchini Pie

DRINK
8. Lemonade with Crunchy Pomegranate Seeds

DESSERT
9. Perfect Tri-Color Ice Cream

Recipes by Henry Margaritis and Tom Kukoly

Pizza Dough

Each recipe makes 6 pizzas

Quick-and-Easy Pizza Dough

This recipe can also be used for breadsticks. Just brush with garlic butter, sprinkle with sesame seeds and garlic salt, and cook on a pizza stone (indoor or outdoor) for about 10 minutes at 415°F.

1 1/2 cups warm water, about 110°F
2 1/4 tsp active dry yeast (about 1 envelope)

2 tsp olive oil
2 tsp honey*
2 tsp sea salt*

3 1/2 to 4 cups bread flour,* plus more for dusting

Neapolitan Pizza Dough

This is an authentic Neapolitan pizza dough recipe from VPN Americas. It is a very traditional recipe that requires about six hours of resting time and is best cooked in an outdoor pizza oven. It makes a pizza crust that is finer, with crunchy overtones.

2 1/2 cups room temperature water
1/4 tsp (.04 oz) fresh active yeast (comes in cake form; found in refrigerator section)

1 1/2 Tbsp (.9 oz) sea salt
4 cups (2 lb) type "00" flour,* plus more for dusting

- In a large mixing bowl, combine water and yeast; for quick-and-easy recipe, add olive oil and honey. Set aside for 5 minutes, or until yeast starts to bubble, then add salt.

- Add 1/3 to 1/2 cup of the flour; use your hands to swirl the mixture until all the lumps are dissolved. Add the remaining flour and mix with your hands until the dough starts to pull away from the sides of the bowl.

- Transfer to a floured work surface and knead for 5 minutes, adding flour occasionally, until dough is smooth and no longer sticky. For Neapolitan recipe, knead for 15 minutes total.

- Turn dough into bowl, cover with plastic wrap, and put in a warm area. Let quick-and-easy dough double in size, about 1 hour. For Neapolitan recipe, let rest for 2 hours.

- Place dough on a work surface and divide into six 9-oz balls. Place each ball in its own bowl and cover with plastic wrap. For quick-and-easy recipe, let rest for 10 minutes, then flatten each to a 6- to 8-inch round. Pizza dough can be used right away or saved for later, wrapped, in the refrigerator. For Neapolitan dough, let rest for 4 hours.

TIPS:

- Adding sugar or honey to a recipe will make the crust darker, with brown sugar making it the darkest. If you are storing your pizza dough in the refrigerator (up to 2 to 3 days), as a lot of pizza parlors do, the sugar provides something for the yeast to feed on during the long resting period. By the time the pizza is actually cooked, there is little to no sugar left.

- Don't use table salt for pizza recipes; it's too fine and salty. Always grab the sea salt or kosher salt.

- Bread flour will yield a crispier crust, and all-purpose flour will render the pizza a bit denser and chewier, closer to the typical American takeout variety.

- The only flour sanctioned by the Neapolitan team is "00" flour, because it has a finer grain and will render a perfect wood-fired crust.

- Using a scale to measure flour is preferable, because its volume can vary by as much as 25 percent.

- Many recipes call for mixing the dough in a mixer with a dough hook. I feel this makes the dough a little denser and less elastic, like a rubber band that only goes so far.

Tomato Sauce from VPN Americas

Makes 4 ½ cups

1 36-oz can San Marzano
  tomatoes, with juice

2 tsp Italian oregano
1 Tbsp kosher salt

1 tsp freshly ground
  black pepper

- Mill tomatoes using a food mill or pulse in a food processor until lightly puréed. Add oregano, salt, and pepper.

TIP: Making sauce with real tomatoes takes under 5 minutes and will give your pizza an authentic, homemade taste. Processed pizza sauce will make any indoor- or outdoor-fired pizza taste salty and commercial.

FORMING PIZZA CRUST

1 (9-oz) ball pizza dough
  (baseball-size)

Flour, for dusting

- Place dough on a lightly floured work surface, flatten and push out from the center with your fingertips, forming a circle.
- Carefully lift the dough, tossing it back and forth between your palms.
- Gently stretch to a 12-inch round, being careful not to tear any holes. Although the dough can be rolled out using a rolling pin, stretching by hand is optimal for a better, firmer crust. An oblong pizza that is uniform in thickness is fine.

Adding water or sprinkles of flour will help make the dough the perfect consistency, but do so in small amounts as you go.

METHODS FOR COOKING PIZZA

Grill

- To cook pizza directly on a grill, preheat to medium and generously oil grill. Place a round of prepared plain, untopped quick-and-easy pizza dough on a well-oiled sheet pan. Slide the dough from pan directly onto grill. Cook for 2 to 3 minutes. Brush the top with olive oil and flip the pizza onto the other side. Remove pizza from the grill to a cool pan. Add tomato sauce, cheese, and toppings, and slide pizza back onto grill. Cook until cheese bubbles, 2 to 3 more minutes.

- If using a pizza stone, place it directly on the grill and cover to preheat, 10 minutes. Then slide precooked crust with toppings onto the stone. Cook until cheese begins to bubble.

Outdoor Pizza Oven

- A classic Neapolitan pizza is made with simple, fresh ingredients at temperatures upward of 800°F, and served on a plate with a fork and knife. This pizza will have the outrageously good charred and smoky flavor you can only get from a wood-burning oven.

- Slide Napolitan pizza dough with toppings onto a lightly floured pizza paddle. Transfer pizza to outdoor oven, rotating several times with a steel peel. The pizza will cook in as little as 60 seconds. For the last 10 seconds, you can lift the pizza with the peel toward the top of the oven to make the top bubble to perfection.

Indoor Oven

- To cook indoors, preheat oven with a pizza stone to 450°F. Sprinkle a piece of parchment paper lightly with yellow cornmeal and place a round of dough on it. Put all sauce and toppings on the dough. Slide onto the stone; cook 8 to 10 minutes.

- You can also precook the dough without toppings for 2 minutes on each side on the stone. Precooking the dough can prevent the middle from getting soggy. It's the best method. Try it.

TIP: A little bit of cornstarch on the stone will make the pizza slide on and off nicely, though we don't recommend using cornstarch with the Neapolitan recipe, because it burns the bottom of the pizza in an 800°F oven.

" *For outdoor pizzas, we prefer grilling the vegetables first. At my home, you'll find a long row of bowls with grilled red onions, corn, pears, and peppers. We add bowls of sliced fresh mozzarella, chèvre, prosciutto, sausage, chopped basil, and even chopped chicken nuggets, so that everyone can make their own.* **"**

Margherita Pizza

Serves 1 to 2

1 (9-oz) ball pizza dough
(baseball size)

½ cup Tomato Sauce (page 65)

½ cup sliced or cubed
mozzarella cheese

1 Tbsp grated Parmesan cheese

4 fresh basil leaves, torn

1 Tbsp olive oil

Kosher salt

- Form the dough as described on page 65. Place tomato sauce at the center of uncooked pizza crust. Using the bottom of a ladle, swirl the sauce from the center to the outer edges of the dough, leaving a ½-inch border.

- Place the mozzarella evenly across the pizza, followed by the Parmesan. Scatter the basil leaves and drizzle with olive oil. As a final touch, toss a pinch of salt over the pizza.

- Cook until done, depending on method you're using (page 66).

Mixed Mushroom, Caramelized Onion, and Fontina

Serves 1 to 2

1 small white onion, chopped

2 Tbsp unsalted butter

4 Tbsp olive oil

1 clove garlic, crushed

2 cups mixed mushrooms, chopped

½ cup white wine

2 tsp chopped chives

1 tsp chopped rosemary

Salt and freshly ground
black pepper

1 (9-oz) ball pizza dough
(baseball size)

1 cup shredded fontina cheese

¼ cup shredded mozzarella cheese

Truffle oil (optional)

- Sauté onions in butter over low heat until they are caramelized, about 45 minutes; set aside.

- Heat 2 tablespoons olive oil and the garlic gently over low heat. Remove from heat and let cool.

- In a separate pan over medium heat, add the remaining 2 tablespoons olive oil; sauté the mushrooms until soft. Deglaze the pan with wine, then cook off the liquid. Add the chives and rosemary, and season with salt and pepper.

- Form the dough as described on page 65. Brush dough with garlic-infused olive oil. Top with fontina and mozzarella cheese. Add caramelized onions, mushrooms, and a little more mozzarella and fontina, and cook until done, depending on cooking method (page 66).

- If you're feeling crazy, drizzle pizza with truffle oil.

Farm Stand Vegetable ✦ Holly's favorite

Serves 1 to 2

2 ears corn

½ bunch of asparagus

½ red onion, sliced

1 cup cremini mushrooms or
    1 large Portabella

1 (9-oz) ball pizza dough
    (baseball size)

½ cup Tomato Sauce (page 65)

½ cup sliced or cubed
    mozzarella cheese

¼ cup grated Parmesan cheese

Salt and freshly ground
    black pepper

- Grill corn, asparagus, red onions, and mushrooms to taste. Cut the corn kernels off the cob.
  Slice the mushrooms.
- Form the dough as described on page 65. Spread tomato sauce on dough.
  Top with mozzarella and Parmesan cheese and grilled vegetables.
- Cook until done, depending on cooking method (page 66).

Prosciutto and Arugula ✦ Henri's favorite

Serves 1 to 2

4 Tbsp extra-virgin olive oil

1 clove garlic, crushed

1 (9-oz) ball pizza dough
    (baseball size)

½ cup sliced or cubed
    mozzarella cheese

¼ cup grated Parmesan cheese

1–1 ½ cups arugula leaves

Salt and freshly ground
    black pepper

3–5 thin slices prosciutto

Truffle oil (optional)

- Heat 2 tablespoons olive oil and the garlic gently over low heat. Remove from heat and let cool.
- Form the dough as described on page 65. Brush with garlic-infused olive oil.
  Top with mozzarella and Parmesan cheese.
- Cook until done, depending on cooking method (page 66).
- Dress arugula leaves in the remaining olive oil and season with salt and pepper.
  Arrange salad on cooked pizza. Drape prosciutto on top. If you're feeling crazy, drizzle with truffle oil.

“ *Chef Henri likes prosciutto draped onto pizza after cooking because he's more authentic (and better trained). I like it cooked on top because the sides curl up and get crunchy. You can even sauté chopped prosciutto in a pan to add a salty topping to any pizza.* ”

White Zucchini Pie

Serves 1 to 2

2 medium zucchini

Salt and freshly ground
   black pepper

2 Tbsp unsalted butter

2 Tbsp olive oil

2 cloves garlic, crushed

1 (9-oz) ball pizza dough
   (baseball size)

$\frac{1}{2}$ cup burratta cheese

$\frac{1}{4}$ cup sliced or cubed
   mozzarella cheese

$\frac{1}{4}$ cup grated Parmesan cheese

- Shred zucchini in a mandoline or by hand. Season with salt, and let sit for 15 minutes. Squeeze out excess moisture.
- Sauté shredded zucchini in butter until soft.
- Heat 2 tablespoons olive oil and the garlic gently over low heat. Remove from heat and let cool.
- Form the dough as described on page 65. Brush dough with garlic-infused olive oil. Top with the burratta cheese and two-thirds of the mozzarella; sprinkle with Parmesan. Scatter sautéed zucchini and remaining small pieces of mozzarella on top, and cook until done, depending on cooking method (page 66).

Lemonade with Crunchy Pomegranate Seeds

Serves 8

1 cup simple syrup (page 25)
1 cup freshly squeezed lemon juice

Grated zest of 1 lemon
Lemon slices, for garnish

8 strawberries, for garnish
Pomegranate seeds, for garnish

- Combine the simple syrup with 4 cups cold water, the lemon juice, and lemon zest.
- Place ice in each glass and a slice of lemon and a strawberry on the rim of each. Place 2 spoonfuls of pomegranate seeds into glass and top with lemonade. Add a fun straw!

" Chef Henri and I argue playfully like siblings in the kitchen. I know he appreciates the apron I got him because he wears it every time he comes over. It reads: 'Funny, I don't remember seeing your opinion in the recipe.' "

DESSERT

Perfect Tri-Color Ice Cream

Vanilla ice cream
Strawberry sorbet

Raspberries
Hershey's chocolate sauce

- Place 1 scoop vanilla ice cream and 1 scoop strawberry sorbet in each small ramekin.
- Place raspberries in a circle around the rim.
- Let the children top with chocolate sauce.

MEXICAN NIGHT WITH KATIE LEE AND THE SURFER CHICKS

RECIPES
* Mahi and Skirt Steak Tacos
1. Cumin-Rubbed Skirt Steak
2. Mahi on the Grill
3. Shaved Napa Slaw
4. Corn Relish
5. Guacamole

DRINKS
6. Katie Lee's Pink Grapefruit Margaritas
7. Holly's Cheladas

DESSERT
8. Katie Lee's Pineapple Coconut Sundaes

Recipes by Katie Lee and Warren Schierenbeck

I first met the Food Network chef and authentic Southern belle Katie Lee in the Atlantic Ocean. We had both started surfing that summer, seeking the healing effects of saltwater waves. Safe to say that the skills we've honed together at our outdoor ovens show more deftness and grace than our stances on a board.

Katie welcomes people from all walks of life to enjoy her cooking—surfers, rock stars, radio shock jocks, and cabinetmakers all find their way to her backyard brick oven extravaganzas, where she fires up everything from pots of local clams and mussels brewed with Long Island white wine, tomatoes, and garlic to glazed summer fruit desserts.

Our community of surfing women—surfer chicks, as they say—met last summer to sample her Southern flair for flavors and simple down-home cooking, when she and our friend Warren Schierenbeck paired together to flame up our Mexican night. Sure, we were lured by the promise of fire-grilled mahi tacos dripping with sweet corn relish and the re-creation of a lime-drenched, salty Chelada drink that we'd shared on a recent surf trip to Mexico. But we stayed, like golfers replaying that glorious nine-iron on the par-four fairway, to reminisce over that one wave we caught in the offshore wind off the Sea of Cortez break.

On the beach or in her backyard, Katie always produces the perfect stage for intimate evenings, where the memories and conversations linger even longer than the flavors bursting off her grill.

Warren Schierenbeck's
Mahi and Skirt Steak Tacos

Serves 12

Prepare grilled mahi and skirt steak, and serve in warm tortillas with Napa slaw, corn relish, and guacamole.

✳ Cumin-Rubbed Skirt Steak

2 Tbsp coffee grounds
2 Tbsp honey
2 Tbsp ground cumin
1/4 cup olive oil

Salt and freshly ground
    black pepper
4 lbs skirt steak

- Combine the coffee grounds, honey, cumin, olive oil, salt, and pepper.
  Coat the steak with the marinade and let sit at room temperature for 1 hour.
- Preheat a grill to high. Grill steaks for 3 minutes on each side for medium rare.
- Let rest for 10 minutes on a platter, then slice into 2-inch portions.

TIP: Keep a cup of water close by, just in case flame-ups occur. Splashing small amounts of water will keep the flames at bay.

✳ Mahi on the Grill

1/4 cup chopped cilantro
1/4 cup chopped parsley
1 clove garlic, minced

Juice from 2 limes
3 Tbsp extra-virgin olive oil

4 lbs mahimahi, cut into
    2-oz portions

- Combine the cilantro, parsley, garlic, lime juice, and olive oil.
  Place the fish in a dish, add the marinade, and marinate for 1 hour in the refrigerator.
- Heat a grill to high. Remove fish from marinade, discarding marinade.
  Grill fish for 4 minutes, then flip and grill 2 minutes more.

TIP: Make sure when grilling fish to use the hottest part of the grill to prevent sticking.

✳ Shaved Napa Slaw

1/2 cup chopped cilantro
1/2 cup vegetable oil
3 Tbsp mayonnaise
Salt and freshly ground
    black pepper

1 large head Napa cabbage,
    shaved thin with knife or
    on mandoline
1 cup shaved red cabbage

- Whisk together the cilantro, oil, mayonnaise, salt, and pepper.
  Pour over cabbage and toss to combine. Reserve in fridge to chill until ready to serve.

To keep tortillas warm, wrap them in a damp towel and pop them in a small cast—iron pan at the back of the grill until ready to serve.

✳ Corn Relish

6 ears corn, husked and blistered
    on the grill
1 jalapeño pepper, charred on
    grill and minced

1 cup cooked black beans
$^1/_2$ cup small-diced red bell pepper
$^1/_4$ cup minced cilantro
$^1/_4$ cup extra-virgin olive oil

Juice from 2 limes
Salt and freshly ground
    black pepper

- Cut corn kernels from cob, then combine all ingredients in a bowl, seasoning to taste with salt and pepper.

✳ Guacamole

6 ripe avocados, pitted
$^1/_2$ cup chopped tomato
$^1/_2$ cup finely chopped
    purple onion
3 cloves garlic, minced

1 $^1/_2$ serrano peppers,
    stemmed, seeded, deveined,
    and minced
$^1/_3$ cup chopped cilantro

3 Tbsp freshly squeezed lime
    juice (about 1 $^1/_2$ limes)
Kosher salt and freshly ground
    black pepper

- In a mixing bowl, mash avocadoes with a fork until chunky.
- Add the tomato, onion, garlic, serrano, cilantro, and lime juice and mix well to combine. Season with salt and pepper and serve immediately.

Don't even think about planning girls' nights without a bright, pink cocktail. It's so retro and corny, it works.

"Entertaining outdoors is my favorite way to have people over to my home: It's casual, creates a family feeling no matter who I'm mixing up, and everyone arrives and leaves in a great, happy mood. Somehow, my recipes taste even better when I cook them on an outdoor flame and we eat them in the fresh air."

KATIE LEE

Katie Lee's
Pink Grapefruit Margaritas

Serves 5

2 limes, cut into wedges
Kosher salt, for rimming
    the glasses

1 cup freshly squeezed ruby red
    grapefruit juice
1 Tbsp superfine sugar

2 cups triple sec
2 cups good-quality
    silver tequila

- Rub the outside rim of each margarita glass with one of the lime wedges. Place some salt in a saucer and twist each rim in the salt to coat.
- Combine the grapefruit juice, sugar, triple sec, and tequila in a pitcher and stir until the sugar dissolves.
- Serve on the rocks, or blend with ice for frozen margaritas. Garnish with lime wedges.

Holly's
Cheladas

This is my favorite drink after a surf session, preferably with chips and guac. The alcohol is very light and the citrus is thirst quenching.

Serves 6

1 cup freshly squeezed
    lime juice

Kosher salt, for rimming
    the glasses
6-pack Pacifico beer, chilled

- Pour 2 tablespoons of the lime juice into one saucer and some salt into another. Dip the rims of the glasses in lime to moisten, then twist in salt.
- Fill glasses with crushed ice, fill one-third with remaining lime juice, two-thirds with beer. Stir and serve.

Katie Lee's
Pineapple Coconut Sundaes

Serves 8

1 pineapple, peeled, cored, and
    cut into 8 rings

1 quart coconut ice cream
    or sorbet

1 cup caramel sauce
8 sprigs fresh mint

- Preheat a grill or grill pan coated with cooking spray to medium-high. Grill pineapple slices for 2 to 3 minutes on each side, until caramelized.
- Place each pineapple slice in an individual serving bowl and top with a scoop of coconut ice cream; drizzle with caramel sauce. Garnish with mint.

GUYS' NIGHT OUT SURF AND TURF

The men on their way to a massive food coma.

We all know the type. The men who can barely fry an egg, and yet when it comes to the grill, they are self-proclaimed masters. The type that once the "grill talk" begins, they just won't shut up. They can't. Their inner caveman kicks in.

When I invited a bunch of guy friends over for a surf-and-turf meal, they were impatient from the get-go. "Do you want me to bring some mesquite or hickory chips for the steaks? Are your steak knives sharp enough, or should I bring my own? Can we get extra of everything so we can compare cooking lobsters and steaks on the outdoor oven versus the traditional grill?" (This was an expensive night for me.)

I promised I'd have all the ingredients waiting (and then some), and we began the cook-off. I still maintain that the fire-fueled memories you create will, in the end, count more than the food. However, on this extravagant night, the collective food coma took over the guys so much so that I doubt they remember the conversation, let alone who was present.

Blame it on the surf and turf, which is, after all, the height of culinary conspicuous consumption.

Brontosaurus Steaks

Serves 8

1 bottle good red wine
1 lb (4 sticks) unsalted butter, at
   room temperature

1 cup chopped parsley
$\frac{1}{4}$ cup coarsely ground
   black pepper

Salt
6 pieces double-cut rib steaks
   from butcher

- Make a sangria butter: Heat the wine in a medium stockpot over medium heat, reducing until it gets syrupy. Combine wine reduction, butter, parsley, pepper, and salt, blending thoroughly with a fork.
- Salt the steaks on both sides. To grill, heat a grill and cook about 7 minutes per side. To cook in an outdoor oven, preheat to 475°F with a large cast-iron pan inside; cook in preheated pan for about 7 minutes per side. To cook indoors, preheat the oven to 475°F. Preheat a large cast-iron pan on stove until smoking. Place steaks in pan and cook in the oven for about 12 minutes on each side.
- Just before you take the steaks out of oven or off grill, put 1 tablespoon sangria butter on each side.
- Remove steaks from pan and allow to rest on a cutting board 15 minutes before slicing.

✐ TIPS:

- Choose prime aged meats; the flavor and overall quality is the best.
- Warren says, "The **magic to steak** is to char it at high heat, and then slow roast it at a lower temp. You can achieve this by moving it closer to and then farther away from the heat source. You can also char it on the grill, then put it inside a 300°F oven until medium rare is reached at 120°F internal temperature. Let it rest for 15 minutes and you'll have a perfect **ruby red** steak."

Jurassic Lobster

Serves 8

1 lb (4 sticks) unsalted butter
4 lemons, cut in half
4 limes, cut in half
1 bunch tarragon

1 bunch thyme
2 (4-lb) lobsters, split in half,
   claws cracked

- Preheat outdoor or indoor oven to 475°F.
- Place $\frac{1}{2}$ cup of the butter, the citrus, and herbs, in cavities of lobsters.
- Place lobsters on a cast-iron pan and cook in outdoor oven for 12 to 15 minutes, or on a baking tray in the indoor oven for 18 to 20 minutes, or until juices coagulate on the tray.
- Melt the remaining butter. Serve lobster with melted butter, bibs, and wipes.

✱ Grill-charred half lemons make the best accompaniment to any outdoor dish. Have several on hand for presentation.

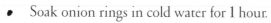

Onion Rings

Serves 8

4 large white onions, cut into
   1-inch rings
1 gallon canola oil
2 cups Wondra flour

1 egg
2 cups seltzer water
3 Tbsp chopped parsley
Salt

- Soak onion rings in cold water for 1 hour.
- Heat oil in 3-gallon pot until it reaches to 350°F.
- Mix flour, egg, and seltzer until just combined. It should look like thin pancake batter.
- Remove onions from water, pat dry, and dredge in batter.
- Fry in batches, taking care not to overcrowd, until golden brown.
- Place on paper towel–lined tray and sprinkle with parsley and salt. Serve immediately.

Creamed Spinach

Serves 8

1 Tbsp olive oil
1 cup diced onion
8 (9-oz) bags of spinach
   (washed)

2 cups whole milk
3 Tbsp unsalted butter
1 Tbsp grated nutmeg

Salt and freshly ground
   black pepper

- Place olive oil and diced onions in a large, heavy-bottom pot over low heat. Cover and cook slowly until soft. Check frequently to prevent burning.
- Add the spinach one bag at a time to let wilt. Then add the remaining ingredients, and cook on medium heat, stirring, until creamy and thick.

> *In a wood oven, the key to keeping lobster meat tender is high heat and bathing the lobster with butter. Keep it moist. Don't be timid.*

WARREN SCHIERENBECK

I love mixing my father up with my male friends. Everyone is so happy in a generational mix.

66 *Treat your men like the rustic, hearty cavemen they are deep down. Let them chomp and gnaw on brontosaurus-size steaks and Jurassic lobsters in a raucous group.* **99**

JULY 4
FAMILY BARBECUE

Fire plays two starring roles at any July 4 barbecue: It is our source of heat for cooking and the entertainment in the skies.

My friend Warren Schierenbeck, a chef with a lifelong specialty in wood-fired ovens, can make anything taste better than you've ever had it before. For the quintessential American outdoor meal, the barbecue, we've injected some special sparks into the traditions your family knows well. Warren made this most American meal pop louder by creating three different twists on the traditional burger and several varieties of ketchup—sweet mango, espresso, and Thai ginger—that instantly elevate anything you pour them on.

At home, the basket with s'mores fixings is never far away from our backyard fire pit. Once made, why not put them on a plate and drizzle smoking-hot fresh July cherries on them the way I do? This adds a firework flash of red to punch up dessert and will make your July 4 crackle both on the table and in the sky.

Fireworks, early versions of which were invented in China beginning around 200 B.C. to scare away evil spirits, came to America via Europeans who had seen them light up the palaces of Russia's Peter the Great and France's Louis XIV. To commemorate the signing of the Declaration of Independence, John Adams wrote to his wife, Abigail, on July 3, 1776, that he was hoping for "Pomp and Parade . . . and illuminations from one End of this Continent to the other from this Time forward forever more."

A hot dog or marshmallow, like pretty much every food out there, tastes better cooked on a flame in the fresh air.

Burgers

German immigrants began serving "Hamburg-style chopped steak" in American restaurants in the mid-1800s, while hot dogs, in their earliest form, were first created around A.D. 60 by Gaius—the cook for the Roman emperor Nero—who exclaimed that he had "discovered something of great importance." He was right about that.

Serves 24

8 lamb burgers
8 pork burgers
8 chicken burgers

24 assorted styles of rolls, such as Kaiser, seeded, potato, and ciabatta

*Dressed-Up Ketchups (make 1 day ahead)
Lettuce, sliced tomato, sliced onion, or desired toppings

Chicken Burgers

2 lbs ground chicken (1 lb breast meat; 1 lb thigh meat)
$1/_4$ cup minced onion
$1/_4$ cup minced parsley
$1/_4$ cup grated Pecorino cheese

Pork Burgers

2 lbs ground pork
1 cup chopped broccoli rabe, blanched
2 Tbsp minced garlic

Lamb Burgers

2 lbs ground lamb
$1/_4$ cup golden raisins
$1/_4$ cup minced fresh mint leaves

- Make the burgers: Mix ingredients for each type thoroughly and form into eight 4-oz patties each (24 burgers total).
- Cook over high heat on the grill to your liking.
- Assemble with assorted rolls, dressed-up ketchups, and choice of toppings.

TIP: The more fat, the juicier the burger. Don't be shy to ask your butcher for lamb meat with more fat and to mix white and dark chicken meat.

*Dressed-Up Ketchups

Thai Ketchup
Makes about 2 cups

2 cups ketchup
$1/_2$ cup rice vinegar
2 Tbsp Thai fish sauce
2 Tbsp soy sauce
1 Tbsp hot sauce, such as sriracha
2 Tbsp minced ginger
1 stalk lemon grass, minced
1 Tbsp packed brown sugar

Mango Ketchup
Makes about 2 cups

1 cup mango purée
1 cup ketchup
2 Tbsp apple cider vinegar
2 Tbsp packed brown sugar

Espresso Ketchup
Makes about 2 cups

2 cups ketchup
2 Tbsp distilled white vinegar
2 Tbsp coffee grounds
2 Tbsp packed brown sugar

- For each ketchup: Place all ingredients in a saucepot and simmer for 45 minutes. Strain Thai ketchup.
- Let stand for one day in the fridge to marry flavors and serve in mason jars.

Thai

Espresso

Mango

Take your condiments seriously.

RECIPES

Chicago Dog and Papaya Dog with Mango Slaw

Serves 12

3 lbs (24) best hormone-free
  dogs you can find
24 potato rolls

Pickle spears
Tomato slices

Celery seeds
*Mango Slaw

- Grill hot dogs until nice and charred on the outside.
- To serve Chicago style: Place dog in potato roll and garnish with pickle and tomato, and sprinkle with celery seeds.
- To serve Papaya style, top with Mango Slaw.

*Mango Slaw
Serves 8

2 Tbsp minced cilantro
1 Tbsp sriracha sauce
1 Tbsp white wine vinegar
1 Tbsp plain yogurt
Juice of 1 lime
Salt and freshly ground black pepper
1 ripe mango, peeled, pitted, and sliced
1/2 cup shaved Napa cabbage

- Whisk the cilantro, sriracha, vinegar, yogurt, and lime juice together in a bowl.
- Add mango and cabbage and toss to combine.

"Serving delicious food to kids is the one time your children unconditionally adore you. Do it often and prepare it together."

S'Mores with Fresh Cherries

Serves 12

✳ Cherry Compote

1 cup pitted extra-ripe cherries
2 Tbsp sugar
1 Tbsp freshly squeezed lemon juice

✳ S'Mores

1 small bag jumbo marshmallows
12 graham crackers
6 bars semisweet chocolate, broken
    into 12 squares

- Make the compote: Simmer ingredients over medium heat until cherries look like molten lava, about 20 minutes. Let rest while you assemble the s'mores.
- Make the s'mores: Blister marshmallows over an open flame and place one on top of each graham cracker and a square of chocolate. Smother with hot compote. Best eaten on a plate.

In my home, the art of the s'more is given great significance and prestige. I always accompany a patiently created s'more with hot, bubbling berry compote.

PIG ROAST IN THE HEAT OF SUMMER

RECIPES
1. Roasted Herb-Brushed Whole Pig
2. Roasted Oysters with Beer and Lime
3. Kale Slaw with Hushpuppy Croutons
4. Mustard Slaw

DRINK
5. Dark and Stormy

DESSERT
6. Flame-Baked Chocolate Chip Cookies

Recipes by Warren Schierenbeck

An outdoor pig roast transforms your dinner affair into a celebration. Echoing Paleolithic times and medieval festivals in Europe, you too can go whole hog in your own backyard—but you'll need some equipment. Namely, a fire-engine-red smoker or a hot box, a magic roasting box known as La Caja China (page 11), which will maximize your chances of serving a pig that's crispy on the outside with juicy, flavorful, tender meat inside.

For our pig roast, Warren Schierenbeck and I added oysters roasted with beer and lime that popped open on their own after we threw them on a grate over our outdoor fire pit (great for those who want to avoid shucking).

Regardless of where the first cooking fire and techniques came from, we all learned in elementary school that roasting an animal over a flame is part of what makes us human. I must admit I was very cautious the first time we tried to cook a whole pig in my backyard. When everyone stayed late until the moon shone bright, I knew we'd done our job well. The kids finished the evening by making chocolate chip cookies in mini cast-iron pans over the fire-pit grate, ensuring our guests left as satisfied and satiated as our caveman ancestors.

Kale Slaw with Hushpuppy Croutons, page 100.

Roasted Herb-Brushed Whole Pig

Serves 10 to 12

1 (35-lb) pig, deboned by
    butcher, with head and
    skin intact
1 (10-lb) boneless pork loin
10 lbs ground pork
Zest and juice of 6 oranges

6 Granny Smith apples, grated
2 cups minced garlic
2 cups rosemary leaves, chopped
2 cups thyme leaves, chopped
1 cup mint leaves, chopped

Mint, rosemary, and thyme
    sprigs, for basting
1 gallon orange juice
3 cups honey
Salt and freshly ground
    black pepper

- Place pig on outdoor table, skin side down, then lay pork loin down the center.
  Evenly divide the ground pork, orange zest and juice, apple, garlic, and herbs across the pig.

- Tie the pig up like a large roast with 5 to 7 strings across the middle.

- Assemble a brush of herbs such as mint, rosemary, and thyme, and tie them to a stick with a string.
  Combine orange juice and honey and brush the pig with the mixture throughout the cooking process.

- Place in a hot box (like the Caja box described on page 11) over a low flame (about 300°F)
  for 8 hours, until thermometer reads 165°F and the skin is nice and crispy.

✎ TIPS:

- You can salt a pig liberally, because it is such a large piece of meat.
- You will have to replace the coals every hour or so: Rake the ashes
  to the side, remove some, discard in a fireproof container, and pour
  new coals on. It's best to heat the new coals in a Weber charcoal
  starter chimney.

Roasted Oysters with Beer and Lime

Serves 8

3 dozen bluepoint or preferred
    oysters, shells cleaned and
    rinsed in cold water

4 bottles beer
6 limes, cut in wedges

- Place grill grate on top of fire pit or preheat oven to 500°F.
- Place oysters on a roasting pan with sides, then pour in the beer.
- Bake for 15 minutes or until oysters start opening. Serve immediately on a platter with lime wedges.

Kale Slaw with Hushpuppy Croutons

Serves 8

Kale Slaw

1 cup buttermilk
2 Tbsp mayonnaise
2 Tbsp minced garlic
Salt and freshly ground
    black pepper

2 large heads dinosaur kale
    (the flatter, darker kind),
    julienned

6 Granny Smith apples,
    julienned
*1 recipe Hushpuppy Croutons

- Whisk together the buttermilk, mayonnaise, garlic, salt, and pepper.
- Place the kale and apples in a large bowl and dress salad to taste. <u>Place croutons</u> on top to keep crunchy or mix into salad to absorb more of the delicious dressing.

* Hushpuppy Croutons

1 cup fine-ground cornmeal
1 cup all-purpose flour
2 Tbsp sugar
1 Tbsp baking powder

1 tsp baking soda
2 eggs
1 ½ cups buttermilk
2 Tbsp unsalted butter, melted

1 gallon vegetable oil
Salt and freshly ground
    black pepper

- Combine cornmeal, flour, sugar, baking powder, baking soda, eggs, buttermilk, and melted butter in a large bowl; the mixture should look like thick pancake batter. Let rest 1 hour.
- Heat the vegetable oil in 3-gallon pot to 350°F. Slowly drop in tablespoon-size balls of batter and let cook until they turn golden brown.
- Remove carefully with a slotted spoon and place on a paper towel–lined platter. Sprinkle with salt and pepper.

Mustard Slaw

Serves 8

1 cup yellow mustard
1 cup extra-virgin olive oil
½ cup red wine vinegar

¼ cup packed brown sugar
4 carrots, julienned
2 zucchini, julienned

2 cucumbers, julienned
1 red onion, julienned
1 cup radishes, julienned

- Whisk the mustard, olive oil, vinegar, and brown sugar together, and mix with the vegetables. Let marinate at room temperature for 2 hours.

DRINK

Dark and Stormy

Serves 6

¹/₂ cup freshly squeezed
   lime juice
¹/₂ cup turbinado sugar

12 oz good dark rum
6-pack ginger beer
6 lime wedges

- Pour the lime juice into one shallow dish and the sugar in
  another. Dip the rim of each highball glass in the lime juice and
  twist into sugar. Fill glasses with ice.

- Pour in the rum and ginger beer.
  Then squeeze the lime on top and enjoy!

DESSERT

Flame-Baked Chocolate Chip Cookies

Serves 8

1 cup (2 sticks) unsalted butter,
   at room temperature
1 cup packed brown sugar
1 cup granulated sugar

2 large eggs
3 cups all-purpose flour
1 tsp baking powder
2 cups semisweet chocolate chips

- Mix the butter and sugars together until creamed. Add the eggs and mix well.
  Combine the flour and baking powder, then stir into wet ingredients. Stir in chocolate chips.

- Bake in greased mini cast-iron pans on a grate over a firepit for 10 to 15 minutes or in oven at 325°F
  for about 15 minutes (adjust cooking time based on fire heat and how gooey or crispy you like your
  cookies). Serve immediately.

When entertaining outdoors, we have to improvise with natural materials to stand as serving areas. Bales of hay are solid, very inexpensive, and make great tables and chairs.

MONTANA BIG SKY ~~CAMPFIRE~~

In big-sky Montana, there's a special chef named Ben Jones who reminds us, "Outdoor cooking comes down to the root of honoring what's around you and how you proceed in everything you are doing." Outdoor entertaining may create more intimate conversations around the flame, but it also brings us closer to the earth.

Ben knows more about cooking on a hearth than anyone I've met. He grew up in southern Oregon in the Rogue River Valley, and his small family tended the land, raised animals, and built their own outdoor oven out of stones from the creek. His mother fed the kids carob instead of chocolate, honeycombs instead of sugar, goat milk from their farm, and they even ground their own flour in a large wheat grinder. By age eight, Ben would catch crawdads and roast them in a cast-iron skillet over a campfire by himself.

Sustainability is a very catchy phrase, but Ben practices it very deliberately as chef of the Paws Up ranch in Greenough, Montana. Here, Ben shares his very special outdoor meals in the hope that we remember to respect and watch over the earth we all share.

Watermelon-Tomato Salad

Serves 4 to 6

1 lb watermelon,
    cut into 1-inch pieces
3–4 yellow, dark red, and
    green heirloom tomatoes,
    cut into eighths
1 cup frisée

1/2 cup fresh basil leaves,
    torn in half
1 recipe Lime Vinaigrette
Kosher salt or fleur de sel and
    freshly ground black pepper

*Lime Vinaigrette

1/4 cup freshly squeezed lime juice
1 Tbsp Dijon mustard
1 cup extra-virgin olive oil

- Make the vinaigrette: Combine lime juice and mustard in a bowl. While whisking, slowly drizzle in olive oil to emulsify.
- Make the salad: Alternate watermelon and tomatoes pieces on a platter. Intersperse basil and frisée across watermelon and tomatoes. Use a spoon to sprinkle the vinaigrette over the salad without drowning the platter; season with salt and pepper.

Baked Beans with Smoked Bacon and Molasses

Serves 8 to 12

2 lbs dried red beans
1 1/3 lb bacon
1 yellow onion, diced small
4 cloves garlic, chopped
1/2 cup yellow mustard

1 cup molasses
1 cup packed brown sugar
1 (12-oz) can tomato paste
2 Tbsp smoked salt

- Soak the beans in enough water to cover, 24 hours. Drain.
- Cut the bacon into 1-inch lardons and cook just until the fat is rendered; reserve the fat.
- In a Dutch oven, sauté the onions and garlic in the rendered bacon fat over medium heat. Add the beans, cooked bacon, and the seasonings. Add enough water to cover the beans and place a tightly fitting lid on top. Cook on stovetop for 4 to 5 hours on low, covered in an oven for 6 to 8 hours at 325°F, or in the coals of an outdoor hearth.

TIP: Remember that enameled cast-iron cookware such as Le Creuset cannot go on or in an outdoor flame. You'll need black cast-iron with a degree rating over 500°F. (See outdoor-cooking-proof brands on page 13.)

Huckleberry Biscuits

Serves 8 to 12

1 lb (4 sticks) cold unsalted
   butter, cut into 1/2-inch dice,
   plus more for pot
2 1/2 cups bread flour

2 1/2 cups cake flour
2 Tbsp baking powder
1/2 cup sugar

1 tsp salt
3 1/2 cups buttermilk
1/2 cup dried huckleberries

- Prepare a fire in a fire pit and let burn until coals are white hot with no flames. Butter a 10-inch Dutch oven.

- In a large mixing bowl combine the flours, baking powder, sugar, salt, and butter using your hands. Mix until the butter is the size of peas, about 5 minutes.

- Add buttermilk and dried huckleberries to the mixture and mix just until the dough comes together about 1 to 2 minutes. Then transfer dough to a clean surface.

- Flour your hands and bring dough together by hand. Fold dough over several times. Pat to a roughly 2-inch thickness.

- Punch out biscuits using a 2-inch round cutter and arrange in Dutch oven; biscuits should touch but not crowd.

- Lower the Dutch oven into a lightly coaled area of fire pit (not raging fire). Cover with lid and coals and cook for 6 to 8 minutes, then check biscuits. Once they have started to brown, replace lid and let sit 5 minutes off-heat. If no browning has occurred, replace lid and add another layer of coals to the lid to help brown the tops of the biscuits, 5 to 7 minutes.

- To cook indoors, brush the tops of the biscuits with melted butter and bake at 350°F for 7 minutes, or until biscuits are golden brown.

Cast-Iron Jalapeño Corn Bread

Serves 10 to 12

1–2 tsp canola oil
1 1/2 cups (3 sticks) unsalted
   butter, at room temperature
1 1/2 cups sugar
9 eggs

2 cups sour cream
4 cups white cornmeal
1 1/2 cups cake flour
1 Tbsp baking powder

1 tsp iodized salt
1/2 cup small-diced yellow onion
3 jalapeño peppers, minced
1 cup shredded cheddar cheese

- Prepare a fire pit as for huckleberry biscuits. Grease a 10-inch cast-iron pan with oil and place in the coals.

- Cream butter and sugar in a large bowl. Beat in the eggs one at a time, with a whisk. Beat in sour cream, scraping sides.

- Add cornmeal, cake flour, baking powder, and salt, and mix to combine. Add onions and jalapeños; continue to mix until combined using your hands or a stiff whisk. Pour batter into the hot cast-iron pan in the coals. Bake until golden brown, approximately 25 minutes.

- Remove from coals and immediately top with the shredded cheese. Serve warm.

- To cook indoors, bake cornbread at 375°F in a preheated cast-iron pan for approximately 25 minutes.

Huckleberry BBQ Lamb Ribs

Serves 4 to 6

Huckleberry BBQ Lamb Ribs

2 1/2 lbs lamb ribs (pork ribs or lamb chops are both acceptable substitutes)

*1 batch Huckleberry BBQ Sauce
Salt and freshly ground black pepper

- Marinate the ribs in half the huckleberry BBQ sauce for 6 to 8 hours.
- Preheat a grill. Over the hot spot, grill the ribs 3 to 5 minutes, until nicely charred on both sides. For medium-rare, leave lamb on grill for another 4 to 5 minutes, until temperature reaches at least 145°F.
- Cut large sheets of aluminum foil and place a rack of ribs inside each.
  Baste liberally with remaining sauce and create a sealed pouch around the rack of ribs.
- Place rib pouches around the outer ring of the grill so the ribs are not over direct flames, or are over very low coals. Close the grill and cook for at least 1 hour.

*Huckleberry BBQ Sauce
Serves 8

8 Tbsp (1 stick) unsalted butter or canola oil
1 large yellow onion, diced small
6–8 cloves garlic, minced
1 fresh jalapeño pepper, minced, with seeds
4 cups seeded, diced tomatoes
2 (12-oz) cans tomato paste

1 cup molasses
1 cup red wine vinegar
1/2–3/4 cup balsamic vinegar
1/4 cup yellow mustard
2 cups fresh or frozen huckleberries
1 cup packed brown sugar
1/2 cup smoked paprika

1/2 cup ground coriander
2 Tbsp freshly ground black pepper
1 Tbsp smoked salt
1 Tbsp ground cumin
1 Tbsp cayenne pepper
1 tsp ground cloves
1 cinnamon stick

- Heat the butter or oil in a heavy-bottom 8-quart pot over the coals (or medium heat on the stove). Sweat the onions, garlic, jalapeño, and diced tomatoes until soft. Add tomato paste, molasses, red wine and balsamic vinegars, mustard, huckleberries, brown sugar, spices, and 1 cup water; stir to combine. Bring to a simmer.
- Brush some of the coals away, to reduce the heat, to reduce the mixture to a very slow simmer. Cover and cook for at least 3 hours, stirring every 15 to 20 minutes to ensure no scorching occurs. If the sauce looks like it is drying out, add 1/2 cup water, as needed. You may have to add or reduce coals to reach the best temperature.
- Remove cinnamon stick and give mixture a good stir. Taste and adjust seasoning as needed and serve.

The sauce is a little time consuming
but worth the wait!

Hot Coal Rainbow Trout

Serves 4

4 rainbow trout, heads and fins on, pin bones out
Kosher salt and freshly ground black pepper
8 sprigs fresh thyme, plus 2 Tbsp fresh thyme leaves, chopped

2 lemons, sliced
2 yellow peppers, julienned
2 red peppers, julienned
1 cup julienned Walla Walla or other sweet onion

1 cup diced tomato
2 Tbsp finely chopped garlic
2 Tbsp finely chopped shallots
4 Tbsp unsalted butter
1 cup white wine

- Prepare a bed of coals in a grill or campfire.

- Lay each trout on a sheet of aluminum foil that is three to four times the size of the fish; shape foil in a boat shape so liquid doesn't leak out. Season the insides of the fish with salt and pepper. Stuff each trout with 2 sprigs of thyme and sliced lemons. Close the fish back up and top with the remaining thyme, peppers, onions, tomatoes, garlic, and shallots, and season with salt and pepper. Place 1 tablespoon butter on each fish and pour $1/4$ cup of wine on each.

- Fold the foil around the fish to create a seal across the top, crimping into a straight seam across the length of the fish. At both ends, fold the foil up so it creates two handles.

- Place each packet directly into the coals and cook for 15 to 20 minutes. The skin on the coal side will be crispy.

TIP: Always have a bucket of water or sand on hand to extinguish the fire.

Pine needles in the air, crystal-clear flowing rivers at our feet, and the freshest trout we ever did catch landed an hour later on the hot coals.

DESSERT

Triple Berry Cobbler

You can make the filling and topping indoors and then heat the cobbler in mini cast-iron skillets outside.

Serves 8

1 lb frozen blackberries, whole
1 lb frozen blueberries, whole
1 lb frozen raspberries, whole
2 cups cornstarch

2 cups confectioners' sugar
2 Tbsp vanilla bean paste
3 1/2 cups (7 sticks) cold unsalted butter

1 cup all-purpose flour
1 cup rolled oats
2 cups granulated sugar
1 tsp salt

- Toss the frozen berries, cornstarch, confectioners' sugar, and vanilla bean paste together, and place in a large, heavy saucepot with 1 cup (2 sticks) butter. Slowly bring to a boil, stirring frequently. The berries will release their juices and the mixture will begin to thicken as it cooks.

- Taste the filling after 30 minutes. The cornstarch needs to be cooked out, which takes about 1 hour, so be careful not to scorch the bottom! If it does scorch, stop stirring, transfer to a clean pot, and start cooking again on a lower heat.

- Meanwhile, make the topping: Preheat the oven to 350°F. Combine the flour, oats, sugar, and salt in a food processor; pulse to mix. Add the remaining butter, half a stick at a time, pulsing once or twice before each addition. The last half stick should be very cold and cut in by hand with a fork or knife. The mixture should look mealy or grainy.

- Sprinkle topping on a rimmed baking sheet and bake for 15 to 20 minutes, until golden brown.

- To serve, divide the hot berry filling among serving dishes and immediately sprinkle with the topping.

DESSERT

Peach Upside-Down Cakes

Serves 4 to 8

1 lb (4 sticks) unsalted butter at room temperature, plus more for pans
8 ripe yellow peaches

2 1/2 cups sugar
9 eggs
4 cups sour cream
1 Tbsp vanilla bean paste or extract

3 3/4 cups cake flour
2 Tbsp baking powder
1 Tbsp iodized salt

- Prepare hot coals in a grill or fire pit. Butter eight 6-inch cast-iron skillets.

- Slice peaches and arrange on the bottoms of the skillets.

- Cream butter and sugar in a large bowl. Blend in the eggs one at a time; blend in sour cream and vanilla. Incorporate all dry ingredients, and mix for 1 to 2 minutes.

- Place skillets in hot coals, and once the peaches begin to sizzle and cook, pour 1 1/4 cups of the cake mixture into each skillet. Skillets should not be more than halfway filled.

- Cook on hot coals for 5 to 7 minutes to sear the bottoms of the cakes.

- Pull pans out of coals carefully and place very close to fire to finish the tops of the cakes, rotating frequently (do not leave unattended), 45 to 60 minutes.

TIP: This dessert requires well-seasoned cast-iron skillets, but you can also use regular cake pans in an oven. To cook indoors, place skillets in 350°F oven for 10 minutes to cook the peaches a little. Remove and pour in 1 1/4 cups batter; bake 20 to 25 minutes, or until a toothpick inserted in the middle comes out clean.

ALI WENTWORTH'S CRAB BOIL ON THE DOCKS

Hunting for crabs in shallow bays is a favorite tradition of comedian Ali Wentworth's and mine, so we tied string on some chicken drumsticks and caught a barrelful for our Sunday family meal. Ali, whose Mayflower ancestors gave her the pedigree to author *The WASP Cookbook*, planned our clambake on the docks of the Pridwin Hotel in Shelter Island. Her mother, Muffie (no joke), passed down her crab dip recipe.

An outdoor seafood boil is much easier to execute on a protected dock than on an open beach. Less sand in your shoes and on your food, for starters, and a bay will have less wind than the ocean, so your hair and plastic cups, not to mention hot embers, aren't flying around. Presumably, if you forget the wine opener, there's a kitchen nearby, and a stable surface for your table is built into the scene. You can actually steam the crabs anywhere you like, over an oven or on a big outdoor flame, but the corn in this chapter is a perfect example of summer alchemy at its best: a wood-fired, Dos Equis— and mayo-slathered succulent crunch of summer joy.

RECIPES
1. Ali Wentworth's WASP Crab Dip
2. Boiled Crabs "Old Bay" Style
3. Warm Potato and Whole-Grain Mustard Salad
4. Mexican Street Corn
5. Fresh Potato Chips

DRINK
6. Tomato-Oyster Cocktails

DESSERT
7. Peach Ice Cream with Mint

Recipes by Warren Schierenbeck with Ali Wentworth's WASP Crab Dip

Best girlfriends since age four, when I used to lie on the top bunk and lean over and scare her just for kicks.

116

Ali Wentworth's
WASP Crab Dip

Serves 10 to 12

2 cups fresh lump crabmeat,
   picked over for shells
1/2 cup mayonnaise
1 Tbsp Dijon mustard

Juice of 1 lemon
1 tsp sea salt
1 tsp freshly ground pepper

1 tsp chopped fresh parsley
1 tsp chopped fresh dill
Triscuits, or cracker of choice

- Combine the crabmeat, mayonnaise, mustard, lemon juice, salt, and pepper in a serving bowl.
- Sprinkle with chopped parsley and dill. Serve with crackers.

Boiled Crabs "Old Bay" Style

Serves 12

1 cup Old Bay seasoning
2 porter beers, or beers of
   your choice
1 cup chopped parsley leaves
1 cup salt
12 blue claw crabs
Lemon wedges, for serving

- Boil 4 gallons water. Add Old Bay, beer, parsley, and salt.
- Add crabs. Boil for 8 minutes, or until they turn bright red. Remove crabs with a strainer, arrange on a platter, and serve with lemon wedges.

TIPS:

- You can also add clams, corn, and potatoes to the mixture.
- Save a little water, and cool it to use as a base for a Bloody Mary.

Warm Potato and Whole-Grain Mustard Salad

Serves 12

3 lbs fingerling potatoes, sliced into thin coins
Salt and freshly ground black pepper
1 small red onion, shaved paper thin on a mandoline
3 cups extra-virgin olive oil
1 cup sherry vinegar
1/2 cup whole-grain mustard
2 Tbsp honey
1/4 cup chopped tarragon

- Place potatoes in cold, salted water and bring to a simmer. Test for doneness 3 minutes after water reaches a light boil. Drain when just tender.
- Whisk together the remaining ingredients and pour over potatoes; stir gently to combine.
- Let stand at room temperature at least 1 hour before serving, to let the flavors marry.

Catching dozens of crabs
with a simple lure of
chicken drumsticks and
twine at our favorite hotel
in Shelter Island,
The Pridwin.

Mexican Street Corn

Serves 12

1 cup mayonnaise
2 Tbsp chopped canned
  chipotle peppers

12 ears corn, husks intact
1 cup grated fresh Mexican cheese
  (such as queso Oaxaca)

½ cup chopped cilantro
Salt and freshly ground
  black pepper

- Blend mayonnaise and chipotle peppers in a blender.
- Peel back the husks from the corn, keeping husks attached to use as a handle.
  Char corn over the grill to your liking.
- Paint corn with the mayo mixture as it comes off the grill.
- Sprinkle with cheese, cilantro, salt, and pepper.

Fresh Potato Chips

Serves 12

5 Idaho potatoes, well washed
1 gallon canola oil

Sea salt and freshly ground
  black pepper
Malt vinegar

- Place a large bowl in the sink and fill with cold water.
  Shave potatoes with a mandoline directly under cold running
  water, dropping slices into the bowl. Change the water four
  times, until no longer cloudy. Drain well.
- Heat oil in 3-gallon pot over medium heat until it reaches 350°F.
  Meanwhile, pat the raw potato slices as dry as you can with paper towels.
- Fry potato chips in batches until golden brown. Do not overcrowd the fryer.
  Remove with a slotted strainer, placing on a paper towel–covered tray.
- Sprinkle with salt, pepper, and malt vinegar to serve.

Tomato-Oyster Cocktails

Serves 6

6 East Coast oysters, shucked, oyster liquor (juice) reserved
6 cups tomato juice
8 oz vodka

1 oz freshly squeezed lemon juice
1 Tbsp prepared horseradish
Freshly ground black pepper

- Place one oyster in each glass.
- Combine the oyster liquor and remaining ingredients in a pitcher, stir, and divide among glasses.

Oyster juice blends the flavors of the sea beautifully into a traditional Bloody Mary.

> *For most people, crab dip is an appetizer. For WASPs, who tend to focus on the Bloody Marys—it's a full meal!*
>
> ALI WENTWORTH

DESSERT

Peach Ice Cream with Mint

Serves 12

4 cups heavy cream
6 large eggs

1 cup sugar
$1/2$ cup mint leaves

6 overripe peaches, pitted and roughly chopped

- In a small pot, simmer cream and sugar until sugar completely dissolves. Remove from heat.
- In a separate bowl, whisk egg yolks. Whisk in one-third of the hot cream. Return mixture to pot, and cook over low heat.
- Gently cook until mixture coats the back of spoon.
- Refrigerate overnight.
- Add to ice cream maker and proceed according to manufacturer's instructions.
- Once ice cream comes together in the machine, finish with the peaches and mint.

IVY LEAGUE GRIDIRON TAILGATE

RECIPES
1. Julia Reed's Hot Cheese Olives
2. Corn Soufflé
3. Brown Sugar Bacon Sticks
4. Pulled Jerk Chicken or Pork Sliders
5. Best Mini Grilled Cheeses Even an
   Ivy-Leaguer Would Leave the Library For
6. Grilled Thai Honey Sriracha Wings
7. Grilled Pizza Dough Hot Dogs
   with Spicy Mustard and Chutney

DRINK
8. Mulled Cinnamon Wine

DESSERT
9. Homemade Cherry or Blueberry
   "Pop-Tarts" (depending on your team)

Recipes by Tom Kukoly with
Julia Reed's Hot Cheese Olives

I go crazy like a 1950s housewife to make sure the tailgate spread is just right.

As autumn's cherry reds and ochres bring this book to a close, I end with a group of fanatics cooking outside for that **uniquely American meal: the tailgate.** As festive as harvest celebrations in medieval times, a tailgate will include feasting, music, and strolling freely among small gatherings and larger groupings behind open car trunks. It's not uncommon to see the bartering of Bloody Marys for burgers among people who have never met—people who see **outdoor cooking as a sport** that rivals any football game.

These enthusiasts take their fare as seriously as any outdoor culinary adventure, and, as proof, it has been noted that 50 percent of tailgaters never actually make it to the game. For this gridiron celebration on a crisp fall day, Tom Kukoly came up with **nonstop action fare** that will enhance the **game-time camaraderie** and community, while crushing the opposition in the next parking slot.

Julia refers to these as her "salt delivery system." She advises, in her very Julia way, to "keep hundreds of those sons o' bitches in the freezer and bring them out anytime you have a crowd."

RECIPES

Julia Reed's Hot Cheese Olives

Makes 50 hors d'oeuvres

8 Tbsp (1 stick) unsalted butter, at room temperature
8 oz extra-sharp cheddar cheese, grated
2 oz Parmesan cheese, grated
1 1/2 cups unsifted all-purpose flour

1/4 tsp cayenne pepper
1/8 tsp salt
1 large egg
50 small pimento-stuffed cocktail olives, drained and patted dry

- Beat the butter in a large mixing bowl until creamy. Add the cheese and mix well. Stir in the flour, cayenne, and salt until smooth.

- In a separate bowl, beat the egg with 2 tablespoons cold water. Add to the dough, and mix just until incorporated. Refrigerate for 30 minutes.

- Preheat oven to 350°F. Remove the dough and flatten out a piece about the size of a walnut into a thin round. Place an olive on top and shape dough around the olive, pinching to repair any breaks. Place it on an ungreased cookie sheet. Repeat with the remaining dough and olives.

- Bake until the dough sets, about 15 minutes. Serve hot.

RECIPES

Corn Soufflé

Serves 10 to 12

3/4 cup (1 1/2 sticks) unsalted butter, at room temperature, plus more for pan
4 eggs
1 cup half-and-half

16 oz sour cream
2 (15-oz) cans creamed corn
1 white onion, diced
1 jalapeño pepper, minced

2 boxes Jiffy cornbread mix
1 Tbsp salt
1/2 Tbsp freshly ground black pepper

- Preheat oven or heat a grill to 350°F. Butter a 8-inch baking dish.

- In a medium bowl, mix together the butter, eggs, half-and-half, and sour cream. Stir in corn, onions, jalapeños, and cornbread mix.

- Pour the batter into the buttered baking dish. Bake for 25 to 30 minutes, or until lightly brown. To cook on grill, cover and maintain a temperature between 300°F and 400°F for 30 to 40 minutes.

Brown Sugar Bacon Sticks

Serves 10 to 12

2 lbs thick-sliced bacon   2 cups packed brown sugar

- Preheat oven to 375°F. Line a rimmed baking sheet with parchment paper or aluminum foil.
- Toss each bacon strip in brown sugar, evenly coating all of the bacon.
  Place bacon strips on prepared baking sheet, making sure they are lined up uniformly and not touching one another. Sprinkle the remaining sugar on top of the bacon.
- Bake for 20 minutes, or until bacon starts to brown. At this point, start checking it frequently, as the bacon can burn easily. Continue to bake until the bacon is super crispy and golden brown, up to 10 more minutes.
- Set aside to cool. This can be stored for several days at room temperature.

Pulled Jerk Chicken or Pork Sliders

Serves 10 to 12

$\frac{1}{2}$ cup freshly squeezed lime juice

2 Tbsp nutmeg

2 Tbsp freshly ground black pepper

2 Tbsp cinnamon

4 Tbsp allspice

4 Tbsp soy sauce

2 Tbsp chopped fresh cilantro

2 jalapeño peppers, chopped

2 Tbsp packed brown sugar

1 cup ketchup

$\frac{1}{2}$ cup malt vinegar

$\frac{1}{4}$ cup dark rum

2 medium chickens, quartered, or 2 lbs pork shoulder

10–12 mini brioche buns, or your favorite rolls

- Transfer all ingredients except for chicken or pork and buns to a food processor.
  Pulse until roughly combined. (This is great to make 3 hours to a day ahead.)
  Use half to marinate the meat, and save the other half to dress it later on.
  Do not mix raw meat marinade with anything you use later.
- For chicken, preheat a grill. Shake off excess marinade from chicken (discarding excess marinade) and grill for about 25 minutes, until meat reaches an internal temperature of 165°F.
- If cooking pork, preheat the oven to 500°F. Place pork shoulder in a roasting pan.
  Roast for 20 minutes. Then reduce heat to 325°F and roast for 4 hours, or until pork is tender.
- Transfer chicken or pork to a bowl. Pull the meat into strips, resembling barbecue.
  Add the remaining marinade.
- Heat the jerk in a cast-iron skillet on the grill over medium heat.
- Serve on buttered, grilled buns.

Best Mini Grilled Cheeses Even an Ivy-Leaguer Would Leave the Library For

Makes 10 Sandwiches

20 slices thinly sliced white bread
*Assorted fillings
1 ¼ cups (2 ½ sticks) butter

*Gruyere with Fresh Sage Leaves

6 oz gruyère cheese
4 sage leaves

*Cheddar Cheese with Onion Jam

6 oz cheddar cheese
2 Tbsp Onion Jam

Onion Jam

4 red onions, sliced
1 Tbsp olive oil
½ cup red wine
½ cup packed brown sugar

- Sauté the onions with olive oil over medium heat in a small pot, 5 minutes. Add red wine and brown sugar, and cook, 20 minutes, until thick and jamlike. Set aside to cool.

*White Cheddar and Brown Sugar Bacon

6 oz white cheddar cheese
4 strips of Brown Sugar Bacon
(page 128)

*Monterey Jack Cheese with Sweet Cherry Peppers and Cilantro

6 oz Monterey Jack cheese
¼ cup sweet cherry peppers

*Mozzarella with Prosciutto and Basil Leaf

6 oz mozzarella cheese
4 oz prosciutto
4 basil leaves

- Make the sandwiches just as you would any old-fashioned grilled cheese, with lots of butter on each side. Grill over medium-low heat until golden brown on each side and the cheese is melted.

- Cut sandwiches in quarters to serve.

TIPS:

- The key to a perfect grilled cheese is to use thick-sliced cheese, about 3 ounces per sandwich.

- To save time, you can cook them at home, and reheat on the grill once you are at the game.

Grilled Thai Honey Sriracha Wings

Serves 10 to 12

$^1/_2$ cup sriracha sauce
$^1/_2$ cup honey
2 Tbsp rice wine vinegar
1 Tbsp sesame oil

1 Tbsp freshly ground
   black pepper
1 Tbsp sea salt

$^1/_3$ cup chopped cilantro,
   plus 1 bunch for garnish
5 lbs chicken wings
2 Tbsp sesame seeds, for garnish

- Combine all ingredients in a medium mixing bowl. Reserve half of the marinade to use later on; do not mix raw chicken marinade with anything you use later on.

- Add the chicken wings to half of the marinade. Store in fridge for 2 to 3 hours.

- Preheat the grill. Shake the excess sauce off the wings (discarding marinade) and grill, 8 to 10 minutes, turning halfway through, to a crispy brown finish.

- Place the chicken wings on a serving platter, and pour the remaining half of the marinade on top. Garnish with fresh cilantro and sesame seeds, and serve.

Sriracha marries perfectly with wings because it hits you all at once: It's sweet, sour, spicy, and infused with garlic. It will give you that pre-game adrenaline rush to make sure you are the fan you always strive to be.

Grilled Pizza Dough Hot Dogs with Spicy Mustard and Chutney

Serves 10 to 12

$1/2$ recipe Quick-and-Easy Pizza Dough (page 64),
    or 1 lb storebought
16 hot dogs or 2 lbs cocktail hot dogs
Olive oil
✳Spicy Mustard
✳Chutney

- Preheat a grill to medium. Roll out the dough and cut into rectangles that are an inch shorter than the hot dogs. Roll the dough around the hot dogs. Brush the dough with olive oil. The thinner you roll out your dough, the better this works.
- Grill for 6 to 8 minutes on each side.
- Serve with spicy mustard and chutney.

✳Spicy Mustard

12 oz Dijon mustard	2 Tbsp sriracha
Juice of $1/2$ lemon	$1/2$ jalapeño pepper, diced

- Mix all ingredients together.

✳Chutney

$1/2$ cup diced mango	$1/2$ cup white wine
$1/2$ cup diced pineapple	vinegar
$1/2$ jalapeño, diced	$1/2$ cup yellow mustard
$1/2$ cup chopped cilantro	2 Tbsp honey

- Place all ingredients in a food processor, and blend until smooth. If a little thick, add a few tablespoons of water.

DRINK

Mulled Cinnamon Wine

Serves 8 to 10

4 cups apple cider	$1/4$ cup honey	Zest and juice of 1 orange
1 (750-ml) bottle red wine, such	2 cinnamon sticks	4 whole cloves
as cabernet sauvignon		

- Combine all ingredients in a pot. Heat over a grill for about 10 minutes, until you have a steady simmer. Serve and enjoy.

Homemade Cherry or Blueberry "Pop-Tarts" (depending on your team)

Serves 10 to 12

1 cup blueberries, strawberries, or cherries, chopped roughly

$^1\!/_2$ cup confectioners' sugar

2 Tbsp cornstarch

2 $^1\!/_2$ cups all-purpose flour, plus more for dusting

1 $^1\!/_4$ tsp salt

6 Tbsp unsalted butter, chilled and cubed

$^3\!/_4$ cup vegetable shortening, chilled

1 egg, beaten

2 Tbsp vegetable oil

*Glaze

- Make the filling: Pour fruit into a pan over medium heat; cook for 5 minutes, until juices start to release. Add sugar and cornstarch, and cook, stirring constantly, 25 minutes. Cook until thick and pasty. Set filling aside to cool.

- Mix flour and salt together in a large bowl. Add butter and shortening, mixing with your fingers until it resembles a coarse meal; you should have some chunks that are not fully dissolved. Measure $^1\!/_2$ cup ice water; stir this in slowly, drizzling a little water at a time, mixing with your hands or a spatula until dough begins to clump.

- Roll out the dough to $^1\!/_8$-inch thickness on a floured work surface. Cut dough into 3 by 5–inch rectangles (two per tart). Place 1 tablespoon filling on a rectangle, then place another rectangle on top. Brush a little egg wash on the edges, and crimp with a fork. Repeat with the remaining dough and filling. Refrigerate until ready to bake or transport. If cooking at the game, try to keep them as cold as possible in a cooler when transporting to the tailgate.

- To save time, you can cook beforehand in your kitchen oven at 350°F for 25 minutes, until golden brown. Once cool, spoon on glaze.

- To cook outside, grease a cast-iron skillet with vegetable oil and cook tarts over medium to low heat for 10 minutes on each side.

* Glaze

$^3\!/_4$ cup confectioners' sugar

1 Tbsp milk

1 tsp vanilla extract

Food coloring (red or blue)

Colored sugar, depending on your team

- Pour the confectioners' sugar, milk, vanilla, and food coloring into a medium-size bowl. Whisk together until it reaches spreadable consistency. If you want it thinner or thicker, you can use less milk or more sugar. Spread glaze on cooled tarts. Sprinkle with colored sugar.

SAFETY

- Keep grills, hot boxes, ceramic cookers, and smokers far away from your garage and home. It's best to cook on concrete, stone, or pebbles to make sure flying sparks or sudden spills don't ignite anything nearby.

- Keep a fire extinguisher and hose near any open flame or outdoor cooking area. Consider installing an extra water line and a hose within range of your outdoor cooking space.

- If you do purchase a ceramic cooker, you must "burp" it regularly or it will cough a fireball in your direction.

- Cooking over an open flame is more dangerous than over a backyard grill. Take the proximity to intense heat seriously, as you will be reaching over flames to grab pots, pans, and those precious fallen ears of spicy mayo-slathered corn. Don't even try to use the tongs and spatulas that work in your kitchen. The Grill Heat Aid brand sells sturdy, heatproof gloves.

- If you're moving your party to a dock, beach, or other open area, remember to bring a potholder, tongs, and a small table to rest the food on.

- Whether at the beach or in the backyard, when you are done, do not forget to let the charcoals or wood cool down completely. Once they are no longer lit, dispose of them in a metal container. Never, ever dispose of ashes close to any structure or in garbage bins alongside your home.

- Check out your local beach's posted rules and regulations for fire in the sand and for putting out fires. If you leave burning embers lightly covered with sand, anyone on the beach could walk over them unsuspectingly after you're gone. (Not to mention any lovers rolling around.)

Cooking with children is my favorite way to keep them around the home hearth. It also prepares them for life: Knowing how to cook the basics is the main ingredient for learning to be confident entertainers. When cooking near flames, we can't be too careful with them.

METRIC CONVERSIONS

Volume

1 tsp = $\frac{1}{3}$ tablespoon = $\frac{1}{6}$ fl oz = 4 ml

1 Tbsp = 3 teaspoons = $\frac{1}{2}$ fl oz = 15 ml

$\frac{1}{8}$ cup = 2 tablespoons = 1 fl oz = 30 ml

$\frac{1}{4}$ cup = 4 tablespoons = 2 fl oz = 50 ml

$\frac{1}{3}$ cup = $\frac{1}{4}$ cup plus 4 tsp = 2 $\frac{3}{4}$ fl oz = 75 ml

$\frac{1}{2}$ cup = 8 tablespoons = 4 fl oz = 125 ml

$\frac{3}{4}$ cup = 10 tablespoons = 6 fl oz = 175 ml

1 cup = $\frac{1}{2}$ pint = 8 fl oz = 250 ml

1 pint = 16 fl oz = 2 cups = 500 ml

1 quart = 32 fl oz = 2 pints

1 liter = 34 fl oz = 1 quart plus $\frac{1}{4}$ cup

1 gallon = 128 fl oz = 4 quarts

Mass

$\frac{1}{2}$ oz = 14 grams

2 oz = 57 grams

3 oz = 85 grams

4 oz = 113 grams

5 oz = 142 grams

6 oz = 170 grams

8 oz = 227 grams

10 oz = 283 grams

12 oz = 340 grams

16 oz = 454 grams

Temperature

450°F = 230°C

425°F = 220°C

400°F = 200°C

350°F = 180°C

325°F = 165°C

300°F = 150°C

250°F = 125°C

225°F = 110°C

INDEX

RECITES

Desserts

Drinks

INGREDIENTS

ACKNOWLEDGMENTS

If we are lucky in our professional lives, a project that is pure joy enters our creative space. I always wanted to produce a book that focused on what makes me happiest in life: bringing my friends and family together outdoors. Casual entertaining means just-showered wet hair, jeans, a big sweatshirt draped on our shoulders, a hot, melted appetizer in one hand, and a colorful cocktail that matches the sunset in the other.

First, a thank you to the many chefs whose magic sparks all over these pages. Tom Kukoly not only served up several chapters of delicious, charred-to-perfection fare, but he helped test every single recipe in the book. Katie Lee made fish tacos sizzle; Ben Jones fired up a perfect Western hearth; Warren Schierenbeck displayed his mastery with an outdoor oven and smoker; Julia Reed whipped up astounding New Orleans fare with her friend Ryan Prewitt and made us laugh the whole time; Henry Margaritis stuffed everyone with crusty Neapolitan pizzas; and comedian and lifelong friend Ali Wentworth met us on the docks to revel in summer and its bounties from farm and sea.

Ross Whitaker is a true artist of photography and made all the menus here pop off the pages. He is delightful, funny, intelligent, and always willing to jump into my production madness headfirst.

Emily Gerard, Trisha Azcarate, Rowena Pumaren, Patrina Poette, and Brendan Meaney all pitched in with valuable production and research help. Stephen Beaumont and Eliza Isenbarger shot the gorgeous scenes in Montana at the Paws Up resort. John Markus, Scott Romanoff, and Jay Peterson deserve mention as obsessive grillers who prompted the project and guided me along. I am grateful for all of your contributions. Many close friends and family willingly showed up at the events and tested the food and drink . . . I don't believe this was terribly rough duty, but I'm grateful for your willingness and game attitude for a party.

Finally, working with Assouline was a creative celebration in itself. My astute and efficient editor, Aurora Bell, made the copy sing cleanly while Jihyun Kim labored hard to make sure the layout was gorgeous. Stéphanie Labeille made sure the word was blazoned out. I'd like to thank Esther Kremer, Camille Dubois, and Martine and Prosper Assouline for believing in this book from our very first meeting. The people at Assouline behave like the news-gathering organizations I grew up with in my career. They are careful, thoughtful, quick, and efficient. On top of all that, they have an added flair for artistic vision and execution that is unparalleled in the industry.

Holly Peterson

ABOUT THE AUTHOR

New York Times best-selling author Holly Peterson is also a former contributing editor for *Newsweek* and an Emmy Award–winning producer for ABC News where she spent a dozen years producing features stories. In addition to two novels, her writing has appeared in numerous publications, including the *New York Times, Newsweek, Vogue, Departures, Elle Décor,* and *Harper's Bazaar.*

CREDITS

© 2016 Assouline Publishing
601 West 26th Street, 18th floor
New York, NY 10001, USA
Tel.: 212-989-6769 Fax: 212-647-0005
www.assouline.com

ISBN: 9781614285168
Editorial director: Esther Kremer
Editor: Aurora Bell
Art director: Jihyun Kim